ONLY
THE EYES
SAY YES

ONLY THE EYES SAY YES

A Love Story

PHILIPPE VIGAND
STÉPHANE VIGAND

Arcade Publishing • New York

FIRST ENGLISH-LANGUAGE EDITION

First published in France under the title *Putain de silence*

Library of Congress Cataloging-in-Publication Data

Vigand, Philippe.
    [Putain de silence. English]
    Only the eyes say yes : a love story / Philippe Vigand,
Stéphane Vigand. — 1st English language ed.
        p. cm.
    ISBN 1-55970-508-6
    1. Vigand, Philippe — Health.   2. Coma — Patients — Biog-
raphy.   3. Vigand, Stéphane.   I. Vigand, Stéphane.
II. Title.
    RB150.C6 V5413   2000
    362.1'9683 — dc21   99-47439

Published in the United States by Arcade Publishing, Inc.,
New York
Distributed by Time Warner Trade Publishing

10   9   8   7   6   5   4   3   2   1

Designed by API

BP

PRINTED IN THE UNITED STATES OF AMERICA

For Stéphane

Contents

Preface to the French Edition

ROUGHLY THREE YEARS AGO, I received a visit from a lovely young woman named Stéphane Vigand, who presented me with a manuscript by her husband, Philippe. Almost a decade earlier, in July 1990, Philippe had collapsed in the street one morning on his way to work. He was in a coma for two months; when he awoke he was totally paralyzed, diagnosed as having locked-in syndrome. His heart and lungs still functioned as before, but he was incapable of any voluntary movement. Yet his brain, they later learned, was intact, just as good as ever.

At first people — including doctors and nurses — thought he was a vegetable, and treated him as such. Finally, his wife realized one day that he was blinking his eyes in answer to her comments and questions, and she suddenly understood he was completely cognizant of everything going on around him. From then on, solely by blinking his eyelids, Philippe managed to communicate and let people know that his mental faculties were unimpaired. It was a slow and painful road back, as he describes, but after several years, alone in front of a special computer that tracked his eye movements, he began to "write" his story.

I knew Jean-Dominique Bauby well, and I knew that his book, *The Diving Bell and the Butterfly,* had dealt with the same illness. But every experience is individual and different, and Philippe's narrative, which is full of hope, retracing his stubborn efforts first to survive then to recover a measure of independence and a place within his family, struck me as profoundly moving. The question constantly in my mind as I read his book was: "What would I have done in his place?"

The first time I met Philippe, I asked him point-blank what his object had been in writing this book. He answered: "First, for my wife. Although I write her every day, there are still things I haven't told her. Second, for my children. There has to be some concrete record of this story, so that later they can be proud of their father. Third, to let my parents and my friends know what the eye-blink code, however slow, is capable of conveying. And, finally, to alter the way others look at me, so that I'm no longer considered a vegetable."

The courage that Stéphane Vigand marshaled under these impossible circumstances also won my profound respect and admiration. She too has come through almost a decade of struggles, of anger, but also of slow progress, buoyed by the certainty that her husband would live and by her determination to form a couple with him. I asked her to contribute her own account of the events. But if the memories of husband and wife often coincide, their experiences of the ordeal differ. Therefore, there are two versions of the story, versions that contradict and complement each other, that call and respond. Together, they form what to me is one of the greatest love stories I have ever known.

Anne Carrière
Paris, 1999

Part One

"Everything is possible."
— Philippe Vigand

The Explosion

O*NE MORNING IN JULY 1990,* as I was walking through the Paris suburb of Neuilly toward my office, I heard a gigantic explosion. Strangely, no one else seemed to have noticed it. My legs, shaking frantically, somehow managed to carry me as far as the terrace of a nearby bistro, where I tried to communicate with the waiter. After some hesitation, he agreed to pass on my haltingly expressed message: to phone my wife and call an ambulance. I could feel myself losing control of my arms and legs. Then I began to lose all sense of time. Everything around me was becoming blurred. Someone handed me a glass of water. I have no memory of the ambulance, but I do remember Stéphane's arrival at the hospital. And also my shouting that I didn't want to die and . . . for God's sake, take out my contact lenses!

Then nothing.

Two months in a coma, then a long awakening during which I gradually came to understand the full extent of the damage.

I am absolutely paralyzed. Only my heart continues to beat and my lungs to breathe. The physical sensations — heat, cold, pain — are also very much with me. And my senses — sight, touch, hearing — are intact.

But as for movement, *none*. None whatsoever. It is as though my body were encased in cement, except for my head. I am no longer able to lift a finger, even to make the simplest gesture, such as scratching my ear. And though I understand, I cannot speak. I am like a well-preserved mummy, minus the bandages. I have even lost the newborn's capacity to swallow.

My brain? It functions exactly as before!

In America, this rare condition is called *locked-in syndrome*. The description is apt enough, with the difference that the walls of this prison have large windows without any bars, through which all the sounds of life can enter. Those felled by locked-in syndrome rarely survive.

Sometimes children close their eyes for a few seconds to try and imagine what it would be like to be blind. To play the game of locked-in syndrome, you would have to learn to have no reaction when some-one steps on your toes, learn to see your own clothes catching on fire without being able to do anything about it, watch a truck barreling down on someone you love and be completely incapable of shouting any warning. Having locked-in syndrome also means learning to accept the fact you can't make the slightest gesture of affection, such as running your fingers through your child's hair.

On the positive side, my eyelids seem willing to respond to the only orders I can give them: to blink. And even that takes an incredible effort.

It's not much, but it will have to do.

But do for what?

Can you imagine living, or more precisely, *wanting* to live, as a quadriplegic, mute and buried alive?

Now, almost ten years after my "accident," I want to tell about my long road back. Now I am able to write these words, after years of only "yes" and "no," like a painter with his palette and brush bring-ing dabs of color to his canvas. In my case, the canvas is a computer screen, and my paintbrush is the pupil of my eye, picked up by a camera, which scans the alphabet (my palette) for the letters it needs.

I want to describe my long rehabilitation, which has been punctuated by stages of hope and despair, tears of joy and pain, and inchingly slow progress.

I want to show how, if your will is strong enough, it is possible to survive. To go on.

And finally, I want to express all I owe to those who have never stopped thinking of me as a living, sentient human being.

A Coma Is a Dream

TWO MONTHS IN A COMA IS A LONG, GENTLE HIATUS, during which the person experiencing it obviously has no sense of time. Two months of which nothing remains but a memory of many dreams, sometimes funny, sometimes tragic, often violent. I was aware that I had received some kind of serious bodily injury, and I sensed that enormous difficulties lay ahead of me.

Everything that had been on my mind before came back to me in a jumbled way: my wife and daughters, my sister, my parents, specific places and concerns of mine at that moment in early summer. our vacation plans, which I knew would have to be postponed.

What struck me was the lack of any logical link

among my dreams. I saw myself as a golf-course designer, busily designing a course on the island of Houat off the Brittany coast, an island I know like the proverbial back of my hand. I was also attending a Michael Jackson concert on that same island, but it was being held not on the beach but on the square in front of the church, which was much too small to contain the tens of thousands of spectators who were arriving from all over the country. The island had been invaded and . . . paralyzed. Therefore I had to leave it immediately. To my surprise, I did not head directly for the Quiberon Peninsula on the mainland directly across from my island, but to the town of La Rochelle, where I had never set foot in my life! The sea was very rough and the spray was drenching us, and I was wondering why there was no roof on the boat. The night, which was very dark, enabled me to admire the fireworks that followed the concert.

What was actually going on around my bed at that moment?

Had someone hooked up a radio? Were they moving my body?

At the port of La Rochelle, my childhood friend, whose name is also Philippe (a.k.a. Chewchew), was waiting for me. Had he just come into the room where I lay comatose? We boarded the train for Paris and ran into Bruno, another close friend. At that time, was he also sitting at my bedside? They had settled me in the far end of the baggage car; I would be more comfortable there.

Then I turned into a building contractor, constructing a magnificent house in the Basque region, a part of the country close to my heart. I reinforced the mansion walls by spitting copiously on them. Was this a premonition of the subsequent dysfunction of my salivary glands?

Even the design of the house seemed to take my paralysis into account, with wide doorways and the rooms all on one level. . . . Could it have been that my wife was talking to me at that very moment about house plans?

Another friend, who was doubtless visiting me in the intensive care unit at the time, invited me into his car, and I found myself all tied up with ropes, meanwhile trying to figure out why it was necessary to tie up a paralytic. Then we were at our house in the Bourbonnais region. As I was incapable of climbing the spiral staircase leading up to my room, I was relegated to an outbuilding near the house. A further premonition? Today that same shed has been converted into living quarters.

In July 1990, the World Cup soccer matches were in full swing. What could be more natural than to have Diego Maradona living with us? And I was extremely upset with the Italian team, whom I suspected of having embedded an object in my brain that made it impossible for me to move. Had the Italians just scored a goal on the French team?

Aware of my disability, I haunted hospital emergency rooms, where I met famous soccer players who had also been injured.

Then my sister Pascale appeared. She was going through difficult labor, giving birth to her daughter. My grandmother was giving her an incredible number of injections, each injection reducing the remaining principal of a loan my grandfather had recently made to her husband. That was probably my way of dealing with all the transfusions I was receiving!

Did I ever wake up? Even for an moment? I have the horrible memory of a dull-eyed male taking care of me in a perfunctory manner, the way you might fill up a vase with fresh water to extend the brief life of cut flowers. . . .

Once again I had become a building contractor. First I had a hospital built at the far end of our little street in the suburbs.

It was still too far away, however, so an apartment was built right next to my hospital room. At times it got so hot there I would slip away to share a beer with some friends.

Finally, I was caught up in a nightmare in the Tronçais forest, where I know every single trail and footpath. I fell into one of the many deep mine shafts that are scattered throughout the forest. The sensation of being dragged down into the abyss is one that still haunts me today. . . .

On several occasions I wanted to give up. My wife was always there to talk me out of it. Was this how I translated to my comatose self the fact that she had been at my side throughout this long voyage?

A Fraction of an Inch per Month

N̲O̲ ̲O̲N̲E̲ ̲E̲M̲E̲R̲G̲E̲S̲ ̲F̲R̲O̲M̲ ̲A̲ ̲T̲W̲O̲-̲M̲O̲N̲T̲H̲ ̲S̲L̲E̲E̲P̲ the way you wake up after a single night. Awareness returns very slowly, as though Nature, in its inscrutable wisdom, had wanted me to become aware only gradually of my new condition. Not unlike the care and sensitivity we display toward those who are dear to us when we are obliged to announce the unexpected death of a loved one.

All I remember of my transfer from the intensive-care unit at Lariboisière Hospital to the unit at Salpêtrière Hospital on Paris's Left Bank are the cobblestones of Paris and the discomfort they caused me. I was put in a room facing south, where I suffered every day from the piercing rays of the sun. The blinds were broken. They probably still are today.

Not yet sufficiently awake to understand why I was there, I had trouble recognizing my wife and parents by sight, although I could make out their voices. My hearing was sharp enough to register the enormous confusion they were feeling and trying to face; I was aware of their doubts about my recovery. Flat on my back, all decked out as I was with a writhing mass of survival tubes, I could guess the questions going through their minds: What shall we do? How shall we do it? When is all this going to end? Is there really any hope?

These were questions that did not faze me in the least. I sensed that something was wrong with my body, but I made no effort to discover what.

To the few people who came to see me, I must not have been a very encouraging sight. I remained motionless, without the slightest physical reaction nor the least sign of understanding. Someone asked me a question; I did not respond.

A woman physiotherapist, who struck me as beautiful, would come in to see me, her visits breaking the monotony of the daily routine. A nurse came to read me poems, her musical voice lulling me to sleep.

Then one day Inspector Columbo showed up, or at any rate his double, wearing the same trench coat and tie. His real name was Philippe Van Eeckhout, a speech pathologist by profession, who was destined to play an important part in this story.

My attitude toward him was the same as it was to all the others: I remained impassive and inert, offering no sign of thought or intelligence. As a result, I could be of no help to him in determining the extent of the damage. The details of my physical condition were pretty clearly established by now, but what of my mental faculties? Had the brain been damaged or impaired? If so, how badly?

Van Eeckhout has since told me that at the time he tended not to accept the diagnoses of the other physicians at face value. They must have judged my chances for mental and physical recuperation as infinitesimal, judging by how often they came to see me.

Van Eeckhout seemed intent on giving me a thorough examination. He spent a long time probing and palpating the living corpse before him. I don't know what prompted him to stick a finger in my mouth, but a sudden spasm caused my jaw to clamp down on it hard, drawing blood! He let out a surprised "Damnation!" which made me burst out laughing.

My reaction took him aback. It was the first indication of a non-vegetative order I had given in weeks, if not months.

The next day he came back and asked me a single question: "Philippe," he said, "tell me, what are two and two?" As my eyelids were the only part of my body I could control, I lowered them distinctly four times.

These four little blinks, seemingly as innocuous as the question that had provoked them, were nonetheless of enormous consequence: they were proof to the world that my mental faculties were neither dormant nor diminished.

For my part, I could see a possible way out: My prison door seemed to open a crack.

And for my family and friends, there was finally proof that I was neither retarded nor mad, nor even mentally impaired. After all those despairing weeks, it was the first sure sign of hope they could latch on to.

From simple arithmetic I soon graduated to answering yes or no questions: one blink for yes, two for no. But this seeming progress quickly proved enormously frustrating: In addition to the fact that my entire body was paralyzed, I had no way of conveying my feelings, my thoughts, or the pain that wracked me all day long. If there was no way I could make myself really understood, then the frustration was destined to become unbearable, my isolation so intense as to defy description.

How can I ever forget the day my wife brought me the means to reconnect myself to the world? One of her friends, a woman named Véronique, had suggested a code we could use, thanks to which I was finally able to express myself again, letter by letter. What was more, the code was one that I could start using immediately, without any training.

After more than two months of silence, I leave it to you to imagine what my first words were. Tell my wife how much I loved her? Say that I wanted to see my daughters Capucine and Juliette, and my parents? That I wanted to live? Know precisely what I was up against from this point on?

None of the above! With great hesitation I blinked out my first sentence: "My feet hurt." In fact, my bed was too short and my feet kept bumping up against the metal bedstead day and night, and hurt terribly.

I can never thank Véronique enough!

Knowing now that I could listen and understand, my entourage was faced with the delicate task of informing me of the nature and extent of my injury, and what my future prospects were.

The first person to try and explain to me why I was paralyzed and unable to talk was a woman whose name I still don't know. I learned that I had two vertebral arteries in my neck and that one of them had spontaneously ruptured, crushing several million nerve cells in the only pathway connecting the brain to the rest of my body. This tiny short circuit had the effect of interrupting all commands between the pilot and his aircraft, though each remained separately intact. I also learned a number of terms I had never heard of before, such as *basilar artery, spinal bulb,* and *cerebral hemisphere.*

And what about my recovery? How long would it take? "A fraction of an inch per month," I was told. As far as I was concerned, my informant was a total ignoramus.

Can hope be measured in fractions of inches?

As for the rest, all the rest, it was not even raised. Comfortably installed and prepared to hear the worst that day, I was spared from having the sky fall on my head. In all likelihood, at that juncture I was incapable of assessing the full impact of my affliction.

My Code and How to Use It

Vowels

	Column 1	Column 2
Row 1	A	O
Row 2	E	U
Row 3	I	Y

Consonants

	Column 1	Column 2	Column 3	Column 4	Column 5
Row 1	B	G	L	Q	V
Row 2	C	H	M	R	W
Row 3	D	J	N	S	X
Row 4	F	K	P	T	Z

Instructions

I always specify first the column of the letter, then its row.

To spell out the name "Peter," for instance, I blink

three times, then four times, indicating the third column, fourth row: P.

E is one blink, then two.

T is four blinks, then four again.

Another E.

R is four blinks, then two.

If the person I'm "talking" to is unsure whether a letter is a vowel or a consonant, they simply ask "vowel or consonant?" and I blink my response.

When people asked me questions, they knew the code would revert to: One blink means yes, two blinks mean no. As time went on and people gained more experience, they could often figure out from the first letter or two what the word would be, thus saving me the time and trouble of having to spell it out completely.

Netter Pavilion,
a Terrible Interlude

*F*OR ANYONE WHO HAS HAD THE UNHAPPY PRIVILEGE
of being struck down by locked-in syndrome and coming out of it alive, the immediate question is: where to
find bed and board? What hospitals are capable of
handling, much less treating, so rare an illness? Few
have any experience in the area, and I think it would
be fair to say that the various medical institutions did
not exactly vie with one another for the pleasure of
having me as one of their patients.

After a great deal of research and several well-
directed telephone calls, Stéphane managed to find me
a bed in the Netter Pavilion at Garches Hospital. I can
remember how impatient I was to be transferred. In

retrospect, the notion of wanting to be sent to Garches now strikes me as more than comical.

Netter Pavilion has a well-earned reputation for putting victims of automobile accidents back together. But my circumstances, I know, were different. Still, it was my ardent hope that a new medical team would be able to work miracles. But that hope was quickly dashed.

Though my code had demonstrated its usefulness beyond all shadow of a doubt, no member of the hospital staff felt impelled to learn it. Worse yet, one of my physical therapists, whose job it was to get me used to being upright again by strapping me to a tilt-table, advised me to relax, go with the flow — this at a time when I was striving for the least sign of hope, determined to make any effort that could possibly be asked of me. His advice was totally unacceptable. And inexcusable.

From that low point on, relations quickly deteriorated further. I was given ice-cold showers. I was left in painfully uncomfortable positions. And I had no way of making myself understood, even on the most basic matters.

Was it because the floor I was on was for brain trauma patients? They were missing all but one or two of their marbles, but they could still talk and shout. On some weekends, with the ward operating on reduced staff, these patients were grouped in the rooms next to mine. I can still hear their shouts and screams filling the night. I thought I was in the loony bin, the only difference being that I was excluded from taking part in the general mayhem.

From time to time, a cortege of white coats filed down the hallway, a professor or two in the lead. Invariably they were trailed by Mrs. X, the director of the department, and several interns, with a bevy of nurses closing the procession. My case must have been a source of entertainment for this prestigious group, since it would pause beside my bed for a long time, watching me like someone in a window display and chatting away merrily. On some days, I felt more like some freak in a sideshow than a bona-fide patient.

Needless to say, these medical visits served no other purpose than to dig a deeper hole in the Social Security system, which was bearing the lion's share of my hospital costs. The only treatment sometimes pre-scribed was a chest X ray. Brilliant! It seemed to me that the bright minds and highly trained individuals in this learned assembly tended to cancel out rather than reinforce one another.

During my first weeks at Garches I got to know another locked-in patient, whose name was Marie-France. I followed her spectacular physical progress with great envy.

Was it because I was mute that the nurses acted like robots when they took care of me? They never made the slightest effort to discover my reactions, although the delicate manipulations they were called on to make required a combination of care and understanding. Only Stéphane, with her sensitivity and intuition, mastered certain of the serious techniques. Reading my eyes, she knew exactly when to stop aspirating the extraneous stuff from my lungs. At those moments, we must both have been thinking what our life together would be like if such aspirations had to be performed several times a day for the next twenty years.

My rare visitors, their minds conditioned by the disabled and unhinged patients they had seen as they came through the ward, often could not conceal their horror and unease. The fact was, I was not an especially attractive sight. A virtual mummy, and to boot one with double phlebitis. What I particularly noticed about their behavior was how hard it was for some to deal with my silence. Those who did not know my code felt they had to adapt to it by speaking in a monologue themselves. A most revealing exercise!

My sense of time was now completely restored: I could see by the calendar on the wall that October 12, the date of my elder daughter Capucine's birthday, was fast approaching. I had invited her, along with her sister, to come celebrate her fifth birthday in the hospital. I had not seen them since my "accident," nor they me. My barely contained joy at the thought of seeing them again was tempered by the fear of how they would react when they saw their father. They whom I had so often escorted across the busy city streets, whom I had lovingly tossed into the air, to the accompaniment of their screams and giggles of real or mock terror, how would they react to me now? In addition to my great happiness at seeing them, I was also hoping their visit might give me a miraculous shot in the arm. I doubtless harbored the notion that strong emotions can sometimes bring about miracles.

From the end of the linoleum-covered hallway I could hear the pitter-patter of their little feet as they trotted all too rapidly toward me. I could feel my heart beating faster.

What I would not have given to prolong those few extraordinarily intense seconds indefinitely!

I had come within a hair of never seeing my daughters again. Yet here they were next to my bed, not nearly as intimidated or as stiff as many adults, and more surprised by my silence, in all likelihood, than by my immobility.

It was their first visit, and they didn't stay long. But any fear I may have had that they would be shocked and damaged was immediately laid to rest. Hospital stays are never much fun, but when you are mute and immobile it can really be hell. By slow degrees I was discovering the meaning of the word "dependency." Unable to move even the tip of my little finger, I had to rely on my family and friends for all the gestures of daily life and began to experience human relations in an entirely different way. Nothing could be done without someone else's help, even in the case of the most trivial needs. It occurs to me that, apart from the first few months of our lives, we are never dependent to this extent; growing up, in fact, is the process of becoming less and less dependent on others.

I had not regressed to infancy, yet, owing to my immobility, the nursing staff tended to treat me as an infant. Does anyone stop to ask a newborn whether he is comfortably installed in his or her bassinet? Nothing is worse than being taken for a baby when you are in your thirties.

I therefore tended to divide all human beings into two categories: those who were willing to understand me and . . . everyone else.

In the first group were, to be sure, those whom Stéphane and my sister Pascale had made friends with in the course of their almost daily afternoon visits. Translating the code, they could convey my basic material wishes, gently pointing out that, crazy as it seemed, even a vegetable might want to change the television channel. Perfect interpreters of my preferences on the subject of pillows or the day's menu, these ladies — whom the afternoon nursing staff dubbed "the Tigresses" — had to be resolute and firm in order to make those willing, or obliged, to come near think of me as a thinking, feeling human being.

As for those in the second category, it was an entirely different matter. For them I was a sack of potatoes. Since I was presumably incapable of a reaction, I was handled roughly or carelessly. To take but one example: When I was dumped onto a rickety gurney for the transfer to Radiology, I had no way of letting the attendants know that a rusty nail was digging into my back on those long rides through the building's clammy and depressing underground passageways. It wasn't until ten months after my accident that Stéphane decided to take a week's vacation, her first since my collapse in the street. In retrospect, I can better understand my terrible feelings of abandonment at the time, since her presence was so utterly indispensable to me. Given the life she had led all those months, she had certainly earned the right to a few days' respite. My parents, sister, and friends had all been duly instructed and given their marching orders; they had received detailed lectures on the procedures and adjustments that gave me a modicum of comfort. All went well. I even had the good taste to greet my wife, upon her return, by raising one of my fingers a quarter of an inch! What an accomplishment! *Not unlike moving a mountain!*

A few days later, I was wedged into a wheelchair

for the first time. Thanks to this excellent invention, I was able to escape the claustrophobic four walls of my cell and breathe the fresh air of the hospital grounds. Long weekends were punctuated by the monologues of friends or family members who were kind enough to keep me company. There were moments of laughter, too, at the astounded looks some of the inmates gave upon catching sight of Pascale's miniskirts, at the nicknames we used (my physical therapist called me "Channel 5" because I was following the early days of this new TV channel with considerable interest) and at the outlandish efforts some of my fellow patients made on the tilt-table trying to wrench themselves free. Most of these patients were accident victims who had suffered severe brain traumas. So impenetrable were their thoughts that they gave the impression they were surrounded by a vast void.

How was the other locked-in syndrome patient, Marie-France, doing? By this time she had progressed to the point of being able to steer her own wheelchair and swallow her food, in contrast to me, who had to ingest it through a demeaning stomach tube. She was even managing to produce a few sounds, whereas my speech therapist could get virtually nothing out of me, any more than could the many apprentices who occasionally replaced her, all of whom were so frightened by my condition they were seemingly incapable of putting any of their hard-earned training and technical knowledge to use. The sounds that issued from my mouth, at the cost of enormous effort, bore little resemblance even to animal sounds, much less human.

Long Live Computers!

THE FACT THAT I HAD MADE no significant recovery left the program's occupational therapist in a quandary. What means could he possibly dream up to give me even a modicum of physical autonomy?

In medical jargon, this is called "adapting the environment to the patient." At about this time, Stéphane was able, basically through family connections, to arrange a meeting with Jean-Luc Lagardère, the head of a publishing and high-technology group that counts among its companies the defense manufacturer Matra. Lagardère had been following my case, partly out of human interest but also because, when I was felled by locked-in syndrome, I had been working for Hachette, one of his companies. He called in the director of research and development at Matra,

Marc Strechinsky. The object: to find a device that would allow me to communicate given the range of movement at my command — which was zero, except for my eyelids.

They decided not to try and develop at Matra what probably already existed elsewhere. Lagardère, citing the war in Vietnam, which had left many U.S. veterans disabled, suggested to Strechinsky that the United States, the leader in developing innovative tools, was the place to look. He entrusted Strechinsky with the task of researching all the recent developments in the field. After paying me a visit at Garches, he also asked Christophe Clément, the occupational therapist, to contact a number of his counterparts in the States.

Three weeks later, they had several promising addresses in hand. The two men set off for the United States and, one contact leading to another, discovered a mom-and-pop business in Virginia run by an engineer who specialized in military technology and his wife, a trained nurse. She had lost her father to locked-in syndrome, and impelled by immediate and pressing need, had performed a number of experiments and developed a computerized device for him.

The way it operates is quite simple. An infrared camera is first trained on your pupil. A control monitor allows you to check that your eye is correctly bracketed by the camera.

You then look at the image of a keyboard on a second monitor, and as your eye comes to rest on individual keys, the word you want is spelled out, letter by letter, as well as the punctuation. Once an entire line has been written, it is saved and appears on a third monitor, which serves as a viewer and is connected to a printer.

You simply look at a character or a function for a half-second and it is selected. Your eye takes the place of a mouse! We christened the machine the "Eyegaze."

At the time, only a few of these machines had been sold. The potential market for them, clearly, is not enormous. One could add: Thank God!

A week or so later, a team of Americans landed in my hospital room, weighed down with equipment, so that I could perform a test run on the system. The test was a great success, except for the fact that I had to turn my head an inch or two in either direction in order to scan the entire alphabet. At the start, it took me twenty minutes to compose a single line, and each letter weighed like a great stone on my head. I could barely bring myself to complete a short sentence. The whole process was so laborious that, at the time, I could not imagine using this barbaric gadget on a regular basis. Still . . .

My first written messages were of course addressed to my wife and children. They were the tangible proof of my love, which I could not voice aloud.

Garches, Part II

As mentioned, garches hospital specializes in the care of accident victims, and the patients there must show that they are making progress. The few improvements I could boast of must not have struck the medical staff as sufficiently significant. We were made to understand that my bed at Garches could be more usefully assigned to someone else.

But where could I go?

Stéphane had managed to wrangle an appointment with the secretary of state for the handicapped, Michel Gillibert, to inquire about the range of options available to the locked-in syndrome patient and also to ask for his support should we need it. His answer was very . . . ministerial. He said he would use his influence to help us set up a care plan specifically adapted to our case. We were delighted. Then less delighted. Then disappointed. Then despairing. No such plan, or help, ever saw the light of day!

My family fought long and hard to find a safe harbor for me. After extensive research, we were convinced that no such place existed. The summer vacation period was fast approaching, and I knew I could not stay on much longer at Garches.

The only possible solution was to go home. Not to our little Paris apartment, which could never house a seriously disabled person, but to the country, where space is at less of a premium. This would mean, however, transporting me almost 200 miles. One bright morning in June an ambulance arrived for me. Stéphane, together with the children, followed close behind in a car, ready, at the first signal from the medics, who were ignorant of my code, to pull up and help. Lying on the stretcher, I tried to follow our route by looking at the treetops filing past. The heat exhausted me, and it took several days for me to recover from the ordeal.

Our stay in the country nevertheless had to be organized along quasi-military lines and depended on the solid goodwill of a number of people simply to provide for the basics. No fewer than four strong arms were needed to seat me in a chair or put me to bed, and it took infinite patience to administer my interminable meals. Someone always had to be present with me, day and night. Not to mention the many and varied operations that required trained personnel.

My return to family life was far from smooth. For the first time my family realized fully how risky and complex a problem it was to have a person with locked-in syndrome staying at home. As for me, I found myself once again in the familiar surroundings I had known prior to my little health problems, surroundings that were far better, and far more comforting, than the hospital.

Offsetting that, the real nature and extent of my disability were now becoming clearer to me. I was party to the clumsy attempts of friends who, wanting to involve me in the activities we once had shared, persisted in filling my ears with their accounts of the forest, the wild animals, their own feats on the golf course. My polite silences often left long voids in the conversation, serving to show once again the difficulty of conversational exchange with someone who resolutely remains mute.

Our country setup was only temporary. In the fall, I would need a well-feathered nest. But despite their many efforts, Stéphane and Pascale could find no roof to give the outcast shelter. School would soon be starting. The children and their mother would have to be heading back to the city.

It was thanks to our friend Alain, a doctor in a clinic at Saint-Amand just outside Paris, that I was able to find a temporary refuge while we continued searching for a facility that would be better adapted to my special circumstances. No longer attended to daily by my two guardian angels, I became entirely focused on the weekends, when Stéphane would be restored to me.

The summer in the country had been beneficial, giving me a much clearer picture of things. I now had few illusions about making a rapid recovery. Furthermore, I decided to stop asking questions such as "when?" and "how long?" Which was a relief to all, both those whose job it was to answer my questions and those responsible for voicing my concerns and anxieties to others.

Fall was upon us, and we had still not come up with a viable solution. Then one day Stéphane showed up at the clinic with a broad smile on her face: Garches Hospital had agreed to take me back. To this day I have no idea what pressures she exerted to make the administration change its mind. My pleasure at finding a solution was offset partially by the sure knowledge that I would lose my guardian angels, except on weekends.

Unable to imagine, much less deal with, the future, I wisely turned my attention to the present. And the present consisted of making life more bearable. On the physical level, this meant training the Garches nursing staff, using my Tigresses as my relentless intermediaries. The various needs of the locked-in syndrome patient are not included in the basic training of your neophyte — or even veteran — nurse. It was my task to let them know the essential details they had to master.

When you are well, you are totally oblivious of the million little gestures you perform unconsciously, simply to keep your body comfortable and in a state of normal equilibrium. These actions, made in response to messages from the brain, are completely mechanical. A person afflicted with locked-in syndrome has no choice but to ask someone else to perform these same gestures for him. Have you ever spent a single night with your hips excruciatingly askew? I guarantee that you'd be unable to fall asleep. Buttocks to the left, shoulders to the right, the head a little bit forward. . . . As my friend Louis says, it's more complicated than tuning up a Formula One racing car! At least when you're not used to it.

Another frustration: going to bed with your testicles caught in a zipper. While on the subject of testicles, if I may, it took several weeks to explain to the physical therapists that they should avoid grabbing me by the belt when hoisting me out of bed, as this maneuver put all my weight on the family jewels. They had forgotten that, though stricken with locked-in syndrome, I was still a man.

I remember my friend Antoine, who was among

my most faithful visitors, once spending over an hour in a valiant effort to find a comfortable position for my head. He was very impressed by two nurse's aides, both named Christiane, who were extraordinarily deft at their tasks. One was slender and blond, the other plump and dark, and they showed great courage and humanity in their unstinting efforts to find a reasonably comfortable position for me, so that I could make it through the long nights without too much pain. By watching and being patient, they had developed an almost infallible method for placing my feet, hips, and shoulders at bearable angles to one another. They also excelled at positioning the six pillows that I need for my head to be comfortable. This one operation could take them anywhere from fifteen seconds to fifteen minutes. Despite the many vagaries of their profession, they never botched the bedtime ceremony. I was so touched by their devotion that my spirits rose and fell according to whether or not they were on duty. They managed to spice up the always insipid meals, and their jokes made me laugh so hard I more than once spattered both their blouses and the walls of my room. I valued them for their company, but also for the warm and intelligent way they dealt with their patients.

Yet they could not be counted on for everything. Stéphane, who believed that appearances can only be allowed to slip so far, noted one day that my hair was filthy. So she found herself with a shower head in one hand, shampoo in the other, and my head propped on her belly. This frothy production earned no more than an ironic glance or two from the day staff.

To make the long weekends at Garches more bearable, I expended vast amounts of energy to see that I was cared for by my favorite nurses. I was in the habit of examining the duty roster every morning to find out who was assigned to the ward. The supervising nurse, who was in charge of filling out the roster, generally allowed patients access to the list. But one Friday when I went into her office with my sister Pascale, the nurse refused to let us look at the clipboard, saying curtly: "The hospital staff does not adapt itself to the whims of patients. Patients are expected to adapt to the hospital organization."

I was furious. And I wanted everyone to know it. My sister, well versed in my code, was ready and willing to translate my answer to the supervisor, letter by letter, in a loud, clear voice.

First letter: B. No comment. Several thousand words start with a B.

Second letter: I. The possibilities were starting to narrow. I could see a smile forming on Pascale's face, whereas the nurse's face was growing grimmer by the second.

Third letter: T. The vulgarity was out.

Fourth letter: C. Now it was clear, but I doggedly

pursued. Pascale was in stitches, and the nurse was deathly pale.

Fifth letter: H.

With a few blinks of my eye I had expressed my full dismay, as well as my anger, at not being understood, at having to live behind a wall I could not break down.

I never saw that supervising nurse again. Whether news of my five-letter word got out or the woman was too embarrassed to face me again and asked for a transfer, I'll never know. That one word, however, had been enough to keep me from ever again being taken as a vegetable.

Chance Meetings

ONE DAY I WAS JUDGED READY to share my room with another patient, a sign of real progress. I'm far from sure those confronted with a locked-in syndrome patient for the first time felt the same way. Among the accident victims who tried living next to an akinetic mute (me) was a young black man who had had the misfortune to dive into an empty swimming pool (a great staple at Garches), but he found our dialogues too unnerving and quickly asked to be moved to another room. Several others followed in his wake; I'll mention only two.

The first was an elderly gentleman named Glacière, or "Icebox," who always complained of being too hot. He was constantly asking to have his face swabbed with a wet washcloth, to the point where none of my visitors could escape the chore. Mr. "Icebox" had been somewhat misled in being sent to Garches, since the hospital only accepts patients who volunteer for rehabilitation, and he adamantly refused any therapy. His wife would come two or three times a week, usually toward seven in the evening. As the time of her visits approached, he would grow more and more nervous and, in his anxiety over her safety on the road, put the entire ward in a state of alarm with his crying, his curses, and his entreaties. When finally she arrived, Icebox would look at her coldly, to all intents completely indifferent, and greet his wife with a nonchalant "Ah! Madame, so glad you could make it! I was starting to get worried!"

Another neighbor, remarkable for other reasons, is someone I will always remember. His name was Maurice Gentilhomme — which one could translate as either "Gentleman" or "Country Squire," depending on the context. Thirty years old, from French Guiana, he was a father of three and an administrator in the postal service at Kourou. An automobile accident had left him paraplegic. Thanks to his courage and willpower, however, he was rapidly able to walk again. He was the only person, during those first years in the hospital, who took the trouble to learn my code. Now I no longer had to wait for the Tigresses to arrive to transmit an urgent message to the staff on our floor. One day, he decided to adopt the role of my personal secretary and call Stéphane so that I could hear her voice. When he tried to put the receiver up to my ear, his legs, as yet not very strong, suddenly gave way. I saw him disappear behind my bed, and, once I had reassured myself he was all right, I was overcome with a fit of uncontrollable giggles, as I kept picturing the expression of wide-eyed surprise on his face as he vanished from view. What a pleasure it was to be able to laugh!

Even now, all these years later, Maurice calls me from time to time from Guiana, where he has returned to his job. He knows all too well what it is to be physically diminished and has a personal and painful understanding of the word "frustration." His wife, who found herself unable to cope with his disability, has left him. I have to say that having a severe disability is not entirely compatible with being the head of a family.

Kerpape, a Perfect Transition

SPRING WAS QUICKLY DRAWING NEAR, once more raising the troubling question of what my future living arrangements would be. Garches had readmitted me on a temporary basis, but again I would have to leave before summer. I could always count on our country house for the summer months, but what would happen afterward?

My sister Pascale was wheeling me through the grounds at Garches, beneath the trees that were just coming into bud. In the course of our "stroll," she began telling me about a rehabilitation center called Kerpape, near the seaside town of Lorient in Brittany. In fact, she said, she had just come back from visiting the facility and had found it especially well-suited to my special circumstances. I was touched by her initiative, but I have to admit that the prospect of being exiled to Brittany did not exactly overwhelm me with joy. For one thing, I would have to deal with several new teams of caregivers, who knew nothing of my "special case," my code, and all the little caring attentions that now made my life physically bearable. I also knew that it would mean I would be moving away from my family and friends for an indeterminate period. In short, the move would be acceptable only if Emmanuel, the young man who had recently signed on as my companion and aide-de-camp during my brief stays away from the hospital, would agree to go with me. He understood me at a glance and could function as my full-time interpreter.

That Stéphane stayed in the background while all this was being discussed and sorted out was no accident: To spare my feelings, she had probably not wanted to give me the impression that she was involved in sending me away.

When I arrived at Kerpape, Stéphane was there to greet me in a big beautiful room with a magnificent view, one that reminded me of the Monterey Peninsula near San Francisco. And this was not the only pleasant surprise. The center's head physician, who turned out to greet us, was completely taken with our eye-blink code right from the start. Later he said that at first he had thought he was at a séance of black magic, surrounded by sorcerers! Could it have been he who ordered the entire staff to learn my code?

After a few hours of somewhat difficult acclimation, the occupational therapist came by to discuss the details of rendering me somewhat independent. The computer and its screens had of course accompanied me to Kerpape, but in his black bag the occupational therapist had something even more useful: a little rectangular box, set on a microphone stand, connected to a handle that is placed in the palm of my hand. By pressing lightly on the handle with the only finger I am capable of moving, I can scroll across the screen a number of functions. By pressing on it a second time, I can choose the function I want — alarm, television, light, radio. I can adjust the volume, change the channel, turn the light on and off, or call for help. So useful and so comforting is this little box that I dubbed it, with good reason, "James." No manservant, however well trained, could have stood me in better stead. From now on I was (slightly) independent. No more lying in agony through an endless night of insomnia because my head or leg was in an uncomfortable position. No more being forced to sit like a prisoner through some insipid radio program or TV movie. Last but not least, my "natural needs" could now be dealt with as they arose, which was a boon to my hospital existence.

★   ★   ★

Since one of my fingers was capable of responding to my commands, why not try out an electric wheelchair? No sooner said than done! The walls of Kerpape still bear the marks to prove my total ineptness at mastering this high-powered rocket, which sometimes, but far from always, obeyed my commands. In fact, more often than not, it seemed to have a mind of its own.

At Kerpape there was a class for handicapped children, which I found almost unbearable to watch — I could so easily imagine my daughters among its pupils. In time, one can perhaps get used to, or accept, the disabilities of other adults, but when the victims are children those same disabilities take on a whole other dimension. The same feeling of utter sadness came over me during a telethon for the benefit of myopathy broadcast from Kerpape a few weeks later.

Pampered as I was by the health-care workers, all of whom as I mentioned had mastered my code, I had hopes that the medical staff itself would show me the same goodwill. My progress depended on it. Life had somehow to be restored to my limbs and vocal cords. But the physical therapists and voice therapists quickly grew discouraged — as a patient, I must not have provided them much motivation. One of the physical therapists was much more interested in Emmanuel's striking resemblance to the French pop star Joe Dassin than he was in restoring life to my poor limbs.

As a result, I abandoned rehab more or less consciously and focused instead on readaptation. Rather than try to recapture a smidgen of my old independence, I was learning to make better use of the tools that had been devised specifically for me. The occupational therapist and the hospital staff were weaving a fabric of which I was a part: For the first time I had the feeling that I was being considered a human being and not a bag of bones. Above all, I was much less sensitive to the feeling of isolation that had weighed on me so heavily at Garches. One marvelous supervisor, aware that her job was to energize rather than supervise, managed to communicate her own smiling good cheer to all the other staff members.

There was also the fact that I finally had a goal: I was no longer condemned to shuttle from hospital to health-care center and back again. Something that would have seemed inconceivable only a few months before was soon going to become a reality — I was going home.

Thanks to the combined efforts of Stéphane and my parents, my little family was going to leave its apartment in the Paris suburb of Neuilly for a house in the nearby town of Levallois, which had been renovated to accommodate a person with serious disabilities. The prospect delighted me, and filled me with all the energy I could muster to solidify my independence. I spent more and more time in front of my writing machine so that I would be ready and able to communicate easily. Above all, I didn't want to be a burden. I tried to fill my lungs with the good sea air of southern Brittany and summoned all my meager resources to avoid swallowing food the wrong way. The resulting spasms, which are terribly upsetting to the uninitiated, occur when even a bit of food fails to find its way to the esophagus and lands in the lungs instead. The lungs strenuously object to the intrusion, and any spectator within range of the subsequent fit of coughing would do well to have an open umbrella at the ready. Painful to me, these displays were unbearable to the cripples in the great dining room at Kerpape, host to a thousand different ways of eating your food without using your hands.

Home to Levallois!

FOR TWO AND A HALF LONG YEARS I had been waiting to go home. The ambulance drivers could never have guessed how insanely happy I was throughout the uncomfortable journey, how jubilant I felt merely at recognizing the various landmarks that signaled our approach to Levallois. As we crossed the neighboring suburbs of Bagatelle and Neuilly, passing under the leafy canopy of those towns' chestnut trees, drawing ever closer to our little street, my emotions grew more and more intense. It was the best journey of my second life!

When I crossed the threshold of the house, I had the impression I was ending a long exile. Stéphane and the children were there to welcome me into this wonderful cave of Ali Baba. *"Le voilà,"* Juliette had cried out upon seeing me. "Here he is." To which her sister replied, playing on the similarity of sounds, *"Le voilà à Levallois!"* — "Here he is at Levallois!"

Everything about the house had been carefully thought out, down to the tiniest details. The halls and doorways were wide enough for my wheelchair, the bathroom was equipped to handle my little infirmities, and the windows of our bedroom looked out onto a small, tree-filled garden.

My ability to act independently and interact with others had also been improved by equipping "James" with additional functions. The signal would now vary according to the floor I was on, so that it would always be easy to find me whenever a problem arose. My sense of isolation vanished as if at the stroke of a magic wand. My only regret was that "James" could not feed me my meals or speak on my behalf.

During the first weeks I spent at Levallois, I must have been very demanding of those around me. I was making up for months of frustration, solitude, silence, and indifference, but I had also unwittingly brought back with me certain habits from the hospital, where everything is, at least in theory, organized around the patient's needs. It is very easy to lose touch with the real world there and forget all the demands to which a healthy, able-bodied person must respond. The atmosphere in our lovely cave therefore sometimes became highly charged. . . . The relationship between

Stéphane and "James" was far from cordial. I could not resist making use of my newfound opportunity to call whenever I wanted to, while my wife was busy coping with other demands. When a mother arrives home from work, she is almost inevitably assailed by her children, who clamor for everything, right away, please, *now!* When she would see me blinking, desperately trying to get her attention by swiveling my head, Stéphane would say: "Can it wait?" And, apart from peeing, everything *could* wait!

I gradually discovered that my contribution to family harmony consisted, at certain times of day, of being totally immobile, avoiding the slightest indication of my presence. When you have locked-in syndrome, you have to know when to fade into the woodwork. A bitter pill! Yet this was the price to pay if family tensions were to return to an acceptable level.

But making yourself into a new person is not easy. Long cut off from my role as a father, I was impatient to resume my place as head of the family. My children had lived without me, grown without me, and had undoubtedly suffered from my exile and from the image I presented at the end of the weekend, when I would cry at having to leave them and return to the white coats at Garches. I was hardly offering them the model of a courageous and exemplary father!

Nevertheless, I *was* the father and husband, and I provided the most constant and regular presence at home. With my observational capacities magnified ten times by my forced inaction, I watched my little world revolve and asked myself what place I might take in it. When it came to messages that could profitably be sent outside the heat of the moment, I spent hours in front of my computer to write a few lines. But when it came to taking part in the crossfire of a conversation, I quickly realized that my interjections were offset in time, therefore useless. A dialogue occurs instantaneously, one utterance displacing another and prompting the next, as each person's ideas take form and are explained. When I lower my head to indicate that I would like to have my say, the thread breaks and the person who interprets my code must make an effort of memory and concentration that temporarily excludes him or her from the debate. By the time I have said my piece, the conversation will have long since gone on to another subject. The time lag is tiring, and I am well aware of a certain irritation among those with whom I most enjoy talking. Nonetheless, I regret that certain of my close friends have never felt bound to make the effort to learn my code, presumably put off by its admittedly esoteric nature. And yet what I may want to report is some piece of crucial information, such as that my son, who has been playing by the window, is now dangling from the ledge, in case they haven't noticed!

★   ★   ★

To celebrate my return to Levallois, Stéphane arranged a surprise party to which she invited everyone who had played a part, large or small, in our saga. Seeing all our friends together gave me enormous pleasure. This was our way of marking the formal end of my hospitalization.

A few weeks later, we held a party for a wider circle, all those who had followed my health problems from a slightly greater distance. This was the first time since my return that I had found myself in a social setting, facing people who had not seen me in almost three years. Most of the looks cast my way undisguisedly seemed to be asking the question "Has the old boy still got all his marbles?"

As a matter of fact, I do have all my marbles! One's intellect and mental faculties can survive a coma and the fog that follows, as well as the various and sundry frustrations attendant thereto. To be sure, the intellect does not obey the law of complementary vessels — less body, more mind — otherwise every seriously disabled person would turn out to be a genius! Paralysis neither impairs nor improves the intellect. The senses on the other hand do develop in new ways, just as the blind develop a more acute sense of hearing than those who can see. I am more sensitive now to others and to the vibrations they give off, feeling it strongly when others are discomfited by my physical presence and my muteness. Only children really appear to feel comfortable, and their candor is refreshing: "Why is that man not walking? Why is that man not talking?"

And so we were celebrating my return, and, at my request, my friend Louis-François was plying me at regular intervals with various forms of alcohol, which he injected via my gastric tube. Although I could taste nothing, I got quite high. Since then I have managed to do without the feeding tube. I now drink sparkling water and, on occasion, a small glass of punch, whose taste I can now appreciate.

That evening marked my return to social life. To compensate for my physical inactivity, I could manage to take part in sessions of intellectual exercise requiring concentration. One such was playing a few rounds of bridge with good friends. So that all would face the same difficulties, the able-bodied were not allowed to sort their hands according to suits, which is how the great champions play. I was able to bid and play my card by simply making a few adjustments to my eye-blink code.

I am also able to dabble in the stock market, though serious investment takes means beyond those at my disposal. And I am able to read books and newspapers, which have to be positioned in front of my eyes on a board and have their pages turned by a helper. All these activities are a happy diversion from watching rebroadcasts of soccer games.

A normal social life includes going out to dinner. Our old van, a converted Renault Espace, can take me and my inseparable wheelchair just about anywhere. And when the elevators aren't working or the elevator door is too narrow for us, I'm carried upstairs on sturdy arms. But the pleasure I derive from these evenings is mixed. I go to them as a partner in a couple, although having locked-in syndrome doesn't heighten your appreciation of social events, particularly if they weren't especially high on your priority list when you were in good health.

The gap between a freewheeling conversation and any interjection of mine is as wide as ever. And when the debate touches on a subject I feel I know well, I may leave my opinion unexpressed, even when the conversation takes a turn I disagree with. On these occasions, it is Stéphane who talks about everything and nothing. Or rather, Stéphane talks about everything while I'm condemned to say nothing! My wife is so dynamic (a friend describes her as a true false-lazybones, in contrast to the false true-lazybones that I am) that her impulsiveness is the antithesis of my enforced calm.

The same delicate gap exists with my children. Only my elder daughter can decipher my code, whereas the two younger children often cannot make sense of the words I have written out for them, especially when they are read out to them more than twenty-four hours after the incident that provoked them. My consolation is to restrict my answers to a single blink for "yes" and two for "no," whereas what children really want to know in general is "Why?" or, more often, "Why not?" I can imagine that some parents must find my forced mutism in such cases most convenient.

The fact that "yes" and "no" are my only linguistic options tends to impoverish my social conversation, and I confess that I pay even less attention to it than I used to.

I am tempted sometimes to break with social conventions.

This is known as the power of the weak.

Today, July 4, 1999, nine years have passed since my accident.

Of course, I think, I love, and I write.

But I still cannot lift a hand.

And I do not speak.

Today, I am truly nostalgic for my old life.

But on the other hand I am grateful to be alive.

Emmanuel, My Double

HAVING LOCKED-IN SYNDROME REQUIRES ME to have a double permanently on hand, someone whose main responsibility is to do for me what I'm incapable of doing myself. And I can tell you that things I can't do for myself are legion. They range from the very simplest, such as turning the pages of a book or news-paper, to the most subtle, such as acting as my inter-preter to all those who do not know my code. That task requires extraordinary diplomacy. The double has to react and intercede without ever overstepping his role as a go-between. He has to become part of the family without becoming a burden, adapt to its rhythm and activities while maintaining a certain dis-tance, without ever abdicating his own personality.

The search for a double is an activity both

Stéphane and I have been engaged in for several years. We have lost count of our fruitless efforts, all those likely seeming candidates who withdrew at the last minute. Drawn from a wide array of nations, even most of those who took on the job found it far too demanding by the end of the second day.

The main object of our search was to find someone to spell Emmanuel, since current labor laws make it illegal to keep a health worker on duty for twenty-four hours a day, seven days a week.

Blessed with a profound and unfailing sense of humor, Emmanuel is kindness personified. At the initial interview, he showed not the slightest trepidation when Stéphane set forth an itemized description of his job responsibilities. And when all the drawbacks of my unregenerate muteness were pointed out to him, he declared, "Don't worry, I'm deaf myself!"

Ever since he came to us in the spring of 1992, he has cracked jokes at the slightest provocation. Street smart, full of beans, he has never for a moment let his professionalism slip. After being my companion for all these years, Emmanuel now has a virtually prophetic sense of what I'm going to say. From the first letter decoded he is very often capable of finishing a word, or even a full sentence, putting it in the very terms I intended to use. His intuition goes beyond reading my mind; it extends to knowing just the right attitude to take with friends, or with people who can't quite figure out how to act when they greet me, often with a pinched air. Emmanuel, who is completely natural, usually manages to dispel whatever unease is in the air and lay the groundwork for a true dialogue. Even if the dialogue rarely lasts for more than twenty-five seconds, that's already a step in the right direction!

It takes enormous sensitivity to create a natural climate around me. When I go out to bring my children home from school, with Emmanuel pushing my wheelchair, not only do my progeny end up on my lap but so do their briefcases, coats, and hats. Thus ridiculously laden, my head tilted at an exaggerated angle, the eternal trail of spittle at my lips, I tend to arouse pity in the hearts of a number of elderly female inhabitants of our neighborhood, who offer me candy that I simply can't refuse, since I come from a long line of stingy Auvergne ancestors. If the kind old ladies only knew how much I long to bite their outstretched hands!

The job of being my double calls for a number of attributes we have found wanting in many of the applicants. One applicant who did perform admirably was a young lady named Danièle. Despite a tendency to be impulsive, she was relaxed, smiling, physically strong, helpful, and generous. Some of my friends also found her "very well stacked," which didn't hurt either. To the fine qualities I have just set forth, we could add many others, such as her habit of sneaking me in some lollipops, which she concealed in her scarf. Danièle, adept at Thai boxing, admires fast cars and big muscles. We also miss her countless, and often bawdy, witticisms, beside which the crude wisecracks of a nightclub performer pale.

These selfless and dedicated assistants do more than replace my motionless arms and legs — they are the actors who allow me to reintegrate myself into a nearly normal existence. Which is saying a lot.

The Way People Look at Me

THERE IS ONE AREA, THOUGH, IN WHICH NATURE has been kind enough to compensate me to some degree for my disabilities: I can almost instantaneously sense and evaluate the looks that others give me.

The game is made all the more interesting by the fact that most people think I don't see, or can't judge, their looks. I find this both funny and pathetic! Using this perceptive talent is my main source of entertainment during those unavoidable family ceremonies — baptisms, weddings, and funerals. I watch the strange dance performed by former friends and distant cousins, who pretend not to see me, who avert their gaze and conspicuously avoid me. Their behavior hurts, of course, but it also makes me uneasy. If they want to gorge themselves at the buffet, fine. If they want to ask the mistress of the house to dance, that I can understand too. But have they pointedly forgotten that we had often sung songs and broken bread together?

It is only one small step from avoiding someone to ignoring them. I remember being invited to a party in honor of a friend's thirtieth birthday. After being carried up to the fourth floor of a building that had no elevator, I found myself plunged into an atmosphere exactly the opposite of the calm necessary for utilizing my code, and I desperately tried to locate, among the strong young men on hand, a few who would still be sober enough to carry me back downstairs at the end of the evening. I had been set down in the middle of the living room like some decorative object. It would have made more sense to post me by the door of the toilet, as a restroom attendant.

Most of the guests didn't know me, and the rest were caught up in vitally important conversations. A few walked up, dripping with kindness and condescension, addressing me in the sugary terms one reserves for infants. I only regretted I was incapable of curling my fingers into a fist!

It must be my immobility that provokes this kind of reaction. The behavior it elicits is sometimes so ludicrous I can't keep from laughing, to the great consternation of those who have taken their courage in both hands to approach me. They thought I had reverted to infancy; now they're convinced I'm completely demented.

"Philippe, remember me? I'm your uncle X! You look just terrific! And isn't he wearing just the loveliest sweater!" Such antics would make me cry . . . if they didn't make me laugh so hard.

In a very short time, I developed a sixth sense for knowing what a person is really thinking, and I can quickly tell if it is along the lines of "What lousy luck!" I also have, on more than one occasion, recognized the terrible look of those who enjoy seeing blood spilled on the road, or a matador gored by a bull, or an ice skater who takes a tumble during his or her exacting program.

My friend Bruno uses an image of concentric circles to explain the degree of closeness of the various people I come in contact with. In the first circle, of course, are my immediate family and close friends. In the second are those who don't know how to deal with me and are wary of, or afraid to, enter an unknown realm. And in the third are all those who take me for a retard.

With a single exception, the eye-blink code is used only by certain members of the first circle. One of my wife's friends, from a very proper family in Versailles, is remarkable for her excellent use of the code whenever we meet, which can hardly be more than twice a year. She at least has understood my need to communicate.

Why should I not be allowed to converse with others and exchange my views? I find it terribly frustrating when Stéphane, in the middle of a noisy crowd, is the only person capable of deciphering my code. She never refuses to do this for me, and often remarks that she has never known anyone who talks and agitates himself as much as I do. Would she like me to express myself even more?

Often isolated during those fierce debates where everyone is talking at once and showing off their culture, wit, and brilliance, I will on occasion remain unperturbed for many long minutes before suddenly allowing my head to fall forward. This gesture signals my intention to break into this remarkably well-informed discussion of the latest book or film to . . . ask: "Excuse me. Could you tell me what time it is?" The comic effect is guaranteed. Unconditionally.

At these dinners, I have the right, because of my physical handicaps, to choose my table partners, and I generally choose men because they are more willing to use my code. But sometimes I will startle my family and close friends by asking that two women be seated next to me on either side. I then pretend I have an unidentified object in my eye and that I need their assistance. At which point I allow them to perch on my lap for as long as it takes to accomplish their rescue mission!

Among the looks I get are those that were cast at me and my wheelchair at Noirmoutier, a seaside resort on the Atlantic coast. What could be more incongruous than a disabled person being pushed along the beach? When I ask Emmanuel to put me into an inflatable boat and I lie there rocked by the waves, I sometimes surprise a tender expression on the faces of the passersby.

My Friends Are the
Best in the World

AFTER AN ACCIDENT SUCH AS MINE, I could very easily have lost all my friends. And yet, I did not. It would be an exaggeration to say that all my friends stood by me, but the fact is, most of them did. In friendship as in love, this is called loyalty.

While I was still in a coma, they kept me company and supported me. Since those days, some have grown even closer. Others have drifted away, such as François, who in the old days was my jogging partner in the Bois de Boulogne; in the long run, he was simply incapable of putting up with the depressing atmosphere at Garches Hospital, or the uninspiring sight of my fellow patients.

The first time I burst out laughing after coming back to life was barely three months after the accident, when my friend Antoine arrived at the hospital and decided to show me the new glasses he had just bought to correct his nearsightedness. The glasses transformed his face in such an unexpected and hilarious way that I practically choked laughing. No one has ever again seen him wearing glasses.

It was when I reached Garches that my visitors began to settle into a regular rhythm. Florence, a charming cousin, as luscious and appetizing as a pastry chef's confection, often came to read at length to me from *L'Equipe,* the daily sports paper, massacring the names of foreign soccer players left and right.

Other than Ghislain and Antoine, who were the first to understand me, the others came to talk and bring me echoes from the outside world.

Now that I am installed at home in Levallois, I receive these friends and a few others at fixed hours, just as our great-grandmothers once did. Bruno comes by every week to keep me up to date on the business world — we worked together in the same firm, and his eldest son Paul is my godson. Ghislain, a busy entrepreneur, still finds the time to keep me company during important soccer matches. Antoine, whom I've already mentioned, gives me the lowdown, in his own inimitable style, on what is going on around the country, drawing on his origins in the province of Berry in central France. He has always managed to keep up a certain "continuity" in our relations, demonstrating that nothing has changed since my accident, except physically. Making me forget my abnormality, he has known how to gauge, with great accuracy, my degree of sensitivity. And by his constant candor he helps me forget, or gloss over, the pitfalls that are part and parcel of my disability.

Finally there is Louis, who shares my passion for the forest and its creatures. These subjects occupy a major share of our lengthy discussions. We like to go over some of our fond memories, especially the visit he made on Christmas day, a year and a half after my accident. He arrived with his girlfriend Marie-Annick to announce that, after several years of fence-straddling, they had at long last decided to get married. We were surprised by their sudden decision, but we wanted to return the Christmas favor and give them an even greater surprise. "And we have something to tell you too," Stéphane announced, and in response to their quizzical looks she told them that she was pregnant. With these two friends we had no need to spell out that I was the putative father!

It is also thanks to friendship that I'm still able to indulge in my love of hunting. Having been exposed to it as a child, I had in my earlier life spent a great deal of my spare time and devoted all my energy to the forest, the dogs, and the animals. I won't even try to explain to the uninitiated the pleasure that some people experience at following after a pack of hounds on the scent of some animal: to fairly understand that thrill, you probably have to have it in your genes. As my genes have survived intact, I continue to race through the underbrush, not as before on foot or on horseback, but with Jean-Louis. A renowned lumberjack, a woodsman of great knowledge, an outstanding hunter of badgers and foxes, he knows every crook and cranny of the forest, where we so often had hunted together.

Years earlier, as I lay on my hospital bed, I often thought on what little chance I had of even remaining in contact with that whole universe. Later on, once I was living in Levallois, I realized there was only one solution: to enlist Jean-Louis, with his boundless energy and his sure, and rapid, sense of decision, to take me back to the woods as a passenger in his 4WD. So together we reentered that lost world, he at the wheel, I in the passenger seat. Shaken and jolted, often bruised, sick after several hours of forest trails, I nonetheless have the impression of staying in touch with the world of hunting and the people who take part in it. All the while he is driving, Jean-Louis keeps up a constant chatter about the latest goings-on in the realm of hunting, as well as all the local gossip. I could never give this up.

As luck would have it, the first time I went hunting after my accident, the hounds went on the trail of the oldest stag in the region. For years I had been trying to watch this magnificent creature through field glasses during the rutting season. That day, the dogs picked out the old stag from a number of others (it is always the weakest that arouses the pack's hunting instinct), showing that it was time for him to be culled. When the stag of La Boulée, for such was his name, was finally brought to bay, all who had followed the hunt were deeply moved. As for myself, I was profoundly saddened by the animal's death: In its most basic and crudest sense, it represented the disappearance of an entire aspect of my life, an aspect of what I had once so loved, one that had so persistently preoccupied me over the years.

I smile now, remembering how my future father-in-law, on the eve of my marriage, confided to his daughter that there was a hidden virtue in my focusing on this passion of mine. Theoretically at least, it would keep me away from any temptation to be unfaithful. Although I've now learned to see my love of hunting in a new perspective, my father-in-law doubtless had a point.

There are two other friends I should also mention, both outrageous enough that they almost cross the line into anarchy. This is probably the reason I like them so much. J.P.V. has never refrained from saying exactly what he thought, without ever worrying about being provocative or "mean."

And then there is Chewchew, my childhood friend, who always does whatever he wants. By definition, he never stays put for very long: He passes through. When he wants to go to bed, he makes no bones about showing his guests the door or slipping away from his hosts the moment the last mouthful is down the hatch. When he is invited anywhere — and he is in great demand because of his conversational talents and good humor — when he feels like leaving he casually mentions that he is dog tired, or has to get up at the crack of dawn, or has a solemn obligation to help his buddy Vigand pass from the seated to the reclining position. Stifling an enormous yawn, I always go along with his white lies.

Sometimes I have the urge to defy convention the way Chewchew does. Yet my respect for Stéphane has prevented me from ever leaving a dinner party before propriety permits. Even at the price of considerable back pain.

By their constancy and generosity, the presence of my many friends is a constant reassurance to my wife that she is not alone in coping with an admittedly burdensome situation. They all play a part in increasing my autonomy and help me reach my main goal — to weigh as lightly as possible on those around me.

A Real Family

AS THE READER WILL HAVE DOUBTLESS FIGURED out by now, when you have locked-in syndrome, there is no way you can live alone. To be sure, there is Emmanuel, my spare pair of arms and legs. But all the same, family relations often take an unsuspected turn. That is probably why I want to write a few lines about those whom my injury has affected most closely. The cross they have had to bear has been totally different from mine. If, as common wisdom has it, one's real self is revealed in the face of hardship, then what my family has shown during this decade-long crisis certainly transcends the heroic.

Is my sister happy? That's a question I have been asking myself for twenty-plus years and, along with everyone else, I'm still looking for the answer. Is there one?

Pascale first married Hervé, a highly ambitious young man from Lyon. She married him despite having a premonition, on the very morning of her wedding, that the marriage was not going to work. Then it was Roger's turn. A brilliant golfer, a bit of a big-time spender, but utterly charming, Roger was very nice — perhaps too nice. They had three children. Pascale's constant shuttling back and forth to my hospital was the immediate cause of — or excuse for — a separation that had long been looming. And finally there is Patrice, a sensitive but moody lawyer — a perfect illustration of the way my sister always seems to go looking for trouble — who currently shares her life.

The situation is complicated, for the very good reason that there is nothing simple about it. We all live at the mercy of the fights and reconciliations between Pascale and Patrice. So rapid are the fluctuations in fact that we often find ourselves a beat or two behind the music. Thinking to arrive at the height of their euphoria, we frequently step straight onto a battle-field. For that reason we have all become cautious in the extreme. And as I myself am in no way exempt from Patrice's sudden mood swings, I conclude that he considers me like everybody else. Bless his heart.

Extremely generous, and utterly devoted, Pascale

threw herself body and soul into the task of helping take care of me during the first two years of my hospitalization. She did not emerge unscathed from the sinister corridors of the Salpêtrière, haunted by a poor man who had lost both his arms and legs in some unknown tragedy, nor from the "Court of Miracles" at Garches and the appreciative tongue-clacking of our brain-damaged comrade in the ward, who would start in the minute he caught sight of her miniskirts. Thus Pascale has had the chance to practice her vocation as a nurse. Like Emmanuel, she learned by doing, and learned very well. Not unlike the praying mantis, she comes to feel proprietary with those she comes into contact with. Since all of this business began, a very deep bond of affection has sprung up between us.

Another "positive side effect" of my accident has been that I have come to better understand my father. Earlier on, we had our share of disagreements, which could in large part be attributed to the generation gap. When I became mute, the quality of our relationship improved greatly. Father is by nature talkative, something of a chatterbox in fact, and monologues suit him admirably. By avoiding sensitive subjects, I demonstrate that I am patient and tolerant. I save the important questions for when I get onto the computer.

When we're together, we often discuss the future, which may appear strange for a man of seventy-six and his quadriplegic son. It seemed to me that my father grew younger when he became more or less convinced that I had come to terms with my new incarnation. I wrote to him one day that you should never let on that you are declining, because advertising your weaknesses — and I know something about this — leaves you open to attacks from all sides.

My mother took my injury as a further challenge, following as it did hard on the heels of the deaths of her father and brother. As there is no ground of shared passions to bring us together (as in the case of my father), my mother brings, to the extent that she is free, all the means at her disposal to make my daily life easier. Without her, certain of the elements that provide "comfort" in my present life would be unthinkable. Constantly thinking of our future, she often leaves to others the task of taking care of the present. All this said, the task of maintaining good relations between my mother and her daughter-in-law is not an easy task. When, as sometimes happens, sparks begin to fly between them, I am forced by my inability to butt in and defuse their conversation to remain on the sidelines. If I decide to intercede using the written word, it takes extraordinary touch to hit on the right combination of humor and firmness. It's not easy to make ice and fire cohabit!

★   ★   ★

My father and mother, stricken as any parents would be by my accident, finally came to accept me as a responsible adult in my new life the day they realized that I was, indeed, fully independent.

Despite his blue eyes, which have been the subject of considerable comment, Pierre is very much his father's son. He was born in June 1992. For the benefit of those who might raise their eyebrows at the date, I can confirm that Pierre was indeed conceived after my accident. And for anyone who might question the ability of a person suffering from locked-in syndrome to fulfill his conjugal duties, I am happy to announce to one and all that my son is not the fruit of any divine intervention on the part of the Holy Ghost.

When one night in November 1991, Stéphane entered my sinister room at Garches, she was clutching in her hand the grainy printout of an ultrasound scan. How my illness was going to turn out was still very much in doubt at the time. But the urge to give life was stronger than anything else, and to me it was an extraordinary proof of resurrection. I was no doubt already projecting, thinking that this child would be able to do everything that I had not had time to accomplish.

Like his father, Pierre lived for a long while in a sitting position. He blinked his eyes in response before he learned to speak. And being of a highly independent frame of mind, he heard only what it suited him to hear. At the age of two, he regularly asked me if he could watch television. Usually I would say no, blinking twice according to our code. But when one day Emmanuel found him glued to the television set despite my prohibition, Pierre replied: "But I'm allowed to today, Daddy *said I could*. In fact, he said 'yes' twice!" How can you fail to be moved by that degree of mischievousness?

Around the same time, the two of us had a near-accident that could have been disastrous. I was waiting in my wheelchair on the sidewalk for Emmanuel to open the door of the house, and Pierre was sitting on my lap. Suddenly, the wheelchair started rolling backward and sent us out into the middle of the heavily trafficked street. Pierre screamed loud enough for both of us, alerting Emmanuel, who whisked us back to the safety of the sidewalk in the nick of time.

My son's numerous whims and antics could sometimes have benefited from the moderating effects of a masculine voice, the voice of a father standing on his own two feet. And as I can wish him neither good morning nor good night, he responds in kind. I cannot kiss him, play with him, or take him to see the animals in the forest. So he responds in like fashion. But Pierre behaves as his sisters do whenever our whole brood are on an outing together, especially when we are surrounded by other people: They never venture far from my wheelchair, and I feel them very close to me, as though it gave them reassurance and stability. The sight of this immobile father, closely surrounded by his offspring, must give pause to anyone tempted to think that, because my body is without movement, my mind must similarly be stripped of all feeling.

Now and then Pierre will raise his voice and tense his little muscles to make clear who is the male animal. His older sisters are sometimes terrorized.

He has the blue eyes of his maternal grandfather and the flat buttocks of his paternal grandfather — buttocks that he is always scratching, his hands plunged into his oversized trousers. To my great disappointment, we are not at the point where we can enjoy watching soccer and rugby games on television together. Maybe that will come later.

There is no evidence that having "a dad on wheels" has been at all traumatic to Pierre. His behavior is normal, down to the risqué songs he sings. I suspect certain of my close friends of profiting from my relaxed surveillance to introduce him to the classics in the genre. He takes advantage of my invalid status to check periodically that my arms and legs are still inert and amuses himself by imitating me when I blink.

Occasionally, after looking through the family photo albums from before 1990, back when his father didn't seem to need Emmanuel and looked like all the other dads, Pierre asks me if I will ever walk again. I tell him that it's most unlikely.

I sometimes go to pick him up from school. He sits on my lap, keeping me warm in winter and protecting me from the sun in summer. I always wait for him away from the press of parents and other children so as not to embarrass him. His school friends have all seen me, and some, I am sure, don't miss the chance to remind him that his father is "strange" or "abnormal."

He collects the little notes I send to him and, although my computer is now equipped with a voice synthesizer, he dislikes its uninflected voice and continues to prefer my written words.

Turning more often and more readily to his mother, he discovered his father's authority during one of Stéphane's absences. I had taken over the responsibility for his daily schedule and for organizing his entertainments. Suddenly dependent on me, he grew much closer.

One day when Stéphane had stepped out to take the girls to school, Pierre slipped into our bed to wait quietly for his wake-up time. We were alone, and I could not have stopped him from drinking a bottle of bleach if he had wanted to. He turned toward me, slowly and questioningly. Then we both smiled at each other. I had the impression then that he understood everything.

A few months later, finding myself behind the closed door of a room from which I could hear all that went on in the house without being seen, I was listening to Juliette and Pierre argue. My son, extremely annoyed at his sister, suddenly burst out: "If you don't stop I'm going to tell Dad!" I cannot tell you the effect that had on me: My efforts had at long last paid off.

Born only a few months before my injury, Juliette has no memory of her able-bodied father. And I for my part missed those fascinating few months when a baby evolves into a child, revealing what her character will be for her entire life. I rediscovered Juliette during the weekends and vacations that I spent away from the hospital, while she struggled to reconcile the fact of having a disabled father with her overall view of the world. A Taurus, with Taurus ascending, always ready to charge ahead, but at the same time shy and sensual, she tends to stand aside from the general flow, though she remains extraordinarily attentive to everything around her. Unshakable in her opinions, she still looks to her loved ones for reinforcement, and in this sense she suffers most from my mutism. Like her paternal grandfather, Juliette needs the approval of others for her thinking to take solid form.

After the death of her great-grandfather, which brought the subject of death to her mind for the first time, she announced to anyone willing to listen: "It doesn't matter whether Dad is handicapped or not, just so long as he's alive!"

It was also Juliette who was most deeply affected by one of my unexpected absences. I had gone to the hospital for a routine half-day exam and had to stay on for a week. Juliette was profoundly upset, thinking that history was repeating itself.

Very curious about the world around her, she asks a thousand mundane questions. Unfortunately, I am unable to help her mother answer them. If by chance I'm the only parent available, Juliette comes up to me, asks the question, then suggests the answer herself. And when there is a choice between two or more options, she always chooses the better solution, surely to avoid my having to object — unless it could be that the effort of decoding my eye blinks strikes her as too strenuous.

My daughter's manner of showing her affection for me has upon occasion nearly ended in disaster. When she had just turned two, I almost choked to death on a baby carrot that she had carefully dug up, washed, then forced into my mouth. She had forgotten that I can only swallow soft foods. Fortunately, Stéphane was not far off and was able to save the day.

And then there was Juliette's pet guinea pig, which everyone in the family was supposed to shower with affection. Lulu, as the animal was known, was left one night lying against my neck. Feeling the call of nature, Lulu deposited a number of tiny turds that worked their way into my tracheotomy. I was able to warn Emmanuel almost immediately, and he delicately removed these objects (whose origin he failed to identify) as they were heading straight for my lungs.

During my periods of hospitalization, when I was only able to return home for short visits, I would always be terribly depressed as the end of my stay approached, like a student heading back to boarding school or a soldier to his barracks after a furlough. And I would bring Juliette back with me in my mind, so that she could keep me company within the walls of my prison. Her little body, round and pink, her curly hair, and the chirpy music of her constant "yeses" all kept me from giving in to depression.

The prison was not outside my body but inside.

Nowadays Juliette, whose maternal instinct at age ten is already well developed, has the capacity to convince herself that she is taking care of me when only a few of us are at home. Despite the reassuring presence of Emmanuel she will, for example, announce authoritatively that she wants to stay with her father, while at the same time her eyes are glued to the TV, watching the same cartoon for the hundredth time, or she is running her fingers lightly over the keys of her piano.

I believe such ringing declarations help Juliette be at peace with herself.

Capucine, our elder daughter, has always startled our friends by her exclusive attachment to me. As soon as she was able to walk, she became my little shadow, refusing to ride on other people's shoulders or be swept up in other people's arms. I think the memory of our walks together in the woods, when I would take her along and share with her my love of animals, is still with her. Eager to pierce nature's secrets, Capucine would concentrate hard to see a motionless stag, a fleeing roe deer, or a fox trotting through the tall grasses. She would quietly put up with the icy winds of February in order to view a frozen pond in the magic of a winter twilight.

There is no returning to these moments of happy complicity. From now on there is one wheelchair too many standing between us.

Since those happy days, our walks have, more typically, been limited to going up and down hospital hallways, with Juliette on my lap and Capucine pushing me, unintentionally mowing down the other, slower-moving cripples.

My injury has accelerated Capucine's natural tendency to be more mature than her calendar age. Never particularly disturbed by my horrible fits of coughing or untimely vomiting, she quickly sought refuge in intellectual activities. At first intrigued by my code, she mastered it very early on, surpassing even some of my close friends in her ability to use it.

In my pre-accident life, I was an ardent soccer fan and had once loved playing as well. I still follow the sport on TV, and Capucine has now become such a fan that she wears a Paris–St. Germain T-shirt when we watch the matches, and badgers me about which is my favorite team, so that she can immediately claim it's hers, too. Her running commentary on the matches, informed by her close reading of the soccer magazines, offers a welcome counterpoint to the commentary offered by the so-called experts.

Wanting always to do more and better — read a few more pages, take off her sweater even when the weather is cold, ride another mile on her bicycle when she has already ridden thirty — Capucine is a staunch advocate of "going as far as you can." This can take the form of pushing family tensions to the breaking point. Perfectly aware of these times when she has gone too far, she will then refuse to interpret the eye blinks I address to her to buttress a well-deserved tongue-lashing from her mother.

Despite their ages, their unsated need for attention and normality, my children have never spoken a hurtful word to me or cast a snide glance my way. Stéphane is to a large extent responsible for keeping their father's image from being diminished or devalued. When they talk to me or ask me a question or look at me, it is not a disabled person they see opposite them but a father.

What is more, it seems that Capucine does indeed admire her father, who, despite all his lousy luck, is on the whole a smiling, upbeat man.

Tarnished Goods

*E*IGHTEEN YEARS AGO, ONLY A SECOND BEFORE I asked Stéphane if she would agree to share the rest of her life with me, I still did not know I was going to pop the question. There was not the slightest premeditation, only a sudden decision, made with the sure knowledge that I had won the jackpot. I was not mistaken, especially in light of the last nine years.

We were married at the tail end of a beautiful summer, and, in the time-honored tradition, we took an oath to love one another "for better or for worse."

And we have indeed known the worse.

For our eighth wedding anniversary, Stéphane had the dubious privilege of explaining the nature of my injury to me, the likely aftereffects, and my chances of ever getting better. I can imagine what courage it took her, first to accept the terrible verdict herself, then to find the words to tell me. My mind being only marginally lucid after the long coma, I was able to listen calmly but without grasping the full extent of the catastrophe. But Stéphane did not walk away scot-free from those two months, during which she sat at my bedside day after day. It was only after the episode of my biting Philippe Van Eeckhout's finger that she could be sure that my mental faculties were intact. That bitten finger not only saved me from the hospice, where I would have been forgotten by everyone within a matter of months; it also marked the end of Stéphane's interminable state of anxiety. At that moment, she needed that ray of hope even more than I.

Because of her, the path we have traveled is extraordinary.

Today, if I had to name something positive that has resulted from my attack, it would be how acutely and profoundly aware I am of the love I bear my wife, not only out of gratitude — if I started to thank her in detail it would take from dawn to dusk — but because I have truly learned the meaning of love.

Stéphane can justifiably complain that she was misinformed about "the goods" she bought: She is constantly faced with the spectacle of a husband with his head bent to the side, spittle dribbling from his mouth, his back and neck twisted grotesquely. I spare myself that same sight by scrupulously avoiding mirrors and any kind of reflecting glass. Could it be a punishment from God? She might well believe it. But punishment for what? It must be something very serious indeed.

Even for a healthy couple, the equilibrium of their shared life is always precarious. In our new life, Stéphane and I have had to make many serious adjustments, and there have been a good many bumps in the road along the way. My growing independence now allows me to roll away from a household scene whenever the situation gets out of hand. As my friend Louis says, a woman's patience is like a rubber band: It stretches and stretches, then stretches some more, but it can suddenly break without warning. So why let matters reach the breaking point? Better off looking for ways to avoid such extremes. Among the meager array of responses available to me for handling household scenes, laughter has always struck me as the best. It took me several months to realize that, after waking up Stéphane a dozen times during the night because of a gurgling tracheotomy (worse than snoring, apparently) or a deafening fit of coughing, the smile I was using to try and put the incident into perspective was more irritating than helpful — the opposite of what I intended.

Faced with so many challenges, Stéphane has had

to make decisions and bring about changes on her own. Her parents are among the few who have had the discretion to know how and when to pitch in during these difficult years, always managing to be available when they were needed to take care of their grandchildren when the situation became intolerable. Never burdensome, they have proved their kindness of heart in so many ways and continue to treat me as a "normal" son-in-law, not as the man who has ruined their daughter's life.

Logically enough, Stéphane's growing independence has kept pace with my own. Over the last several years, she has organized her schedule so she can keep regular office hours. Her employers are most understanding, and if she has to leave work suddenly because one of my nurse's aides has failed to show up or flown the coop, they know why. When I was in the hospital, I was always worried sick thinking ahead to the moment my wife would have to leave. At home, I always wanted to know when she was going to come back. Now I am less concerned, but still happy whenever I hear the front door opening to let her in.

Stéphane continues to plan her life around her children and her husband. She rebuffs any outbursts of kindhearted pity that make me feel inferior: "What a horrible life! How can you stand it?" And she refuses to rank our respective merits — we are in this together, and no one can claim to have heard her complain, not even once. Others take the untactful tack of telling Stéphane that fate dealt her a terrible hand. She would have been just as happy if it hadn't.

It seems to me that we are able to live together because of the pace and energy that Stéphane imparts to everyone around her, as though our linked destinies leave no room for emptiness and nostalgia.

Trust? It is mutual. In any case, my current power of seduction protects me from certain temptations — which doesn't stop me from casting curious and inquiring glances from my wheelchair. My eyes are just as good as ever, and feminine pulchritude just as appreciated, especially since my line of sight is directly on the level of women's well-endowed backsides.

When, for one reason or another, Stéphane has to go out without me, and quite naturally primps as she should before leaving, I have trouble separating her primping from the notion that she is making herself seductive. Nowadays if I find her fetching in her evening wear, it no longer makes me jealous but rather acutely aware of the profound imbalance between her beauty and my Quasimodo-like appearance.

On the contrary, Stéphane seems to feel no embarrassment when out walking with her invalid, reminding him at regular intervals to swallow and sit up straight.

To my wife I owe the fact that I am rehabilitated, rebuilt, "resurrected." And that is a result of her arranging our surroundings so perfectly. Most importantly, I am also indebted to her for having helped me repel — and keep away — the moments of despair.

What Next?

I WAS BORN A SECOND TIME ON JULY 4, 1990. This second life that has been handed to me is so different that it is gradually blotting out the earlier one. I write "handed," because I was never given a choice between accepting or rejecting it. All it takes is a fissure in one little artery for the spinal bulb to be cut off from its blood supply for a few crucial seconds. The consequence is almost always death. In my case, the hangman's rope broke. What makes an artery fissure? No one knows. It can happen as a result of an automobile accident, either serious or trivial; a fall from a horse; blows to the head or neck. But is it really necessary to search for an explanation? The miracle is not so much that the rope broke but that so much distance has been traveled since.

My new existence began on the day I was able to use the eye-blink code and express myself. I blink, therefore I am!

When you emerge from the post-comatose fog to find yourself totally paralyzed and mute, the power of expression is what gives you the energy to overcome your lethargy. It is like a thin trail of air, wafting down to a person trapped under the rubble after a building has collapsed during an earthquake that brings him or her the strength to knock against the walls, however feebly, to try and draw the attention of the emergency crews.

To be sure, the revival of my body has been much slower. Yet how many hours have I spent working to full capacity with speech pathologists and physical therapists! How many men and women of the healing arts have labored, one after the other, to restore life to my limbs and vocal cords! The able-bodied can have no idea the full weight of hope and disappointment contained in these sessions. There was Christian, who was extremely competent but wanted to proceed too fast; and Sandrine, whose hands were oh! so gentle. Some never wanted to learn my code, as though their patient's feelings were of no concern to them. Pierre Moreau has made the effort, and he has been with me for seven years, patiently training all his considerable powers of observation on our work. He knows better than I do what still functions and what might yet show improvement.

But when all is said and done, the results have been far from spectacular. When anyone inquires about my progress, my friend Bruno, half-ironic and half-serious, says I have made none. He is both right and wrong. The progress is imperceptible to many. Those close to me rejoice, as do I, at the slightest gain of even a millimeter over total immobility. These millimeters are matters of indisputable importance to those who battle at my side. As for speech therapy, we may as well not . . . talk about it! With a view toward a possible upturn, I have been developing my breathing capacity with Patrick Tomatis, the renowned yoga teacher.

Whereas before I was completely unable to venture afield more than fifty or sixty miles, I now can go anywhere so long as my backup team is with me. Thanks to the highly perfected system devised by Stéphane for seeing to my material needs, and also to Emmanuel's devotion, I can now participate in crazy adventures. A few years ago, I was able to board a plane, together with my family, to celebrate my fortieth birthday at the Club Med in Sicily, thus proving to Stéphane that I can and will follow her to the ends of the earth, if that is what she wants.

And in the final analysis, what do I have to

complain about? My inertia does not prevent me from enjoying those pleasures that keep me from becoming entirely disincarnate.

One is the pleasure of water and weightlessness, procured for me by my daily bath. Despite the permanent danger of a drop of water somehow finding its way into my lungs, I abandon myself to the nurse's hands. Some nurses understand that their massages transcend the simple function of hygiene; among them is Madame Buchy, who allows these moments to develop their full magic and has no hesitation in prolonging them.

Then there is the pleasure of good food, which I rediscovered once those disgusting paps were no longer pumped directly into my stomach. I never tire of the cooked foods I now eat, though turning them into soft food does to some degree diminish their flavor. But these banquets are frequently interrupted by my swallowing the wrong way, a painful and noisy process that I am still unable to control.

Finally, and most crucially, I still have the love we rediscovered before conceiving Pierre.

Deprived as I am of mobility, I am incapable of any show of the infinite tenderness I would like to impart to our lovemaking — running my hand gently through Stéphane's hair, touching my lips to hers, casting a protective arm around her shoulders. . . . Although the music of words cannot be replaced by a

cold, distant, silent, and sometimes wrongly interpreted code, Stéphane is certainly able to guess what I
would like to whisper to her during these moments of
great pleasure.

The resumption of my normal activities has proceeded
so remarkably that I have even contemplated going
back to work. For instance, my background might
qualify me for a place in government, either in the
Ministry of Agriculture or perhaps in the environ-
mental sector.

For almost a decade I have let others take care of
me. Now it is my turn to take care of others.

The real obstacle is my inability to talk, which is
offset to some degree by the computer and my code.
But only in part, because of the time lag it involves. It
still takes me two hours to write one page, and five
minutes of blinking are equivalent to twenty seconds
of conversation. This constant delay gives rise to
painful frustration. Whenever I start a sentence, I
know exactly where I want it to go, but the same isn't
true of the person I'm talking to, who is as eager as I
am to get to the end of it. Try to imagine a conversation in which one of the participants speaks a word
only every thirty seconds! The rhythm is upsetting to
the person who can speak, who can easily correct
himself, to follow the shifting thread of his thought. I,
on the other hand, am allowed only one try, which

impoverishes any exchange. I therefore go to considerable lengths to choose words I can express, especially given the shortcomings of the code. For instance, there is no provision in the code for the cedilla used in many French words, and once when I was trying to tell a friend about a film I saw and liked, which was entitled *Ransom,* he couldn't for the life of him figure out what in the world I was saying, and asked me whether I was referring to some esoteric Spanish art film. The confusion arose because the French word for ransom is *rançon,* but without the cedilla it looked like Spanish.

People who are lazy, who know only that for me one knock is yes and two is no, often forget that I can't deal with open questions. But you have to know just how to handle them! When someone asks, "Would you prefer going to the movies or the theater?" I obviously can't answer "yes" or "no." Still, I do my best not to be boxed in by the familiar litany of closed questions, which may be easy for my interlocutor but which impoverishes conversation by eliminating the slightest nuance.

The fact that my eye blinks carry no personal inflection sometimes has unexpected results. One day Chantal, a caregiver, deciphered the word "Go." What she understood, given the mood she was in, was "I don't want to see you anymore." What I had intended to convey was that it was high time for her to turn in for the night. She hadn't waited to decode the last part of my message: ". . . and get some sleep!"

These misunderstandings are quickly forgotten when my children's humor enters into the picture. Some time ago, Pierre, who had stayed home alone with me, turned around sharply on hearing a call from my "James" and said: "Don't bother ringing, your wife's not around!"

Before my accident, I tried to juggle my family, my work, and my outside interests. I was devoting only a few Sunday afternoons to my family, with the sinking feeling that I was missing the best part of life. Now at least my accident has set my priorities straight.

Why did everything suddenly change? Now there is no longer any ambiguity about my "case." All the more reason to take care of others while enjoying the wonderful pleasures to be found in the love of family, the proximity of my wife and children, my parents, my sister, my friends. It is their enduring stability that defines the outlines of my existence and the hope it carries.

In a few years, habit will have done its work — we will have forgotten that there was ever a "before." When I conjure up those days, the pain still sears deep inside me.

★　　　★　　　★

Since those pre-accident days, the nature of my feelings has changed: I know no greater happiness than to go "strolling" under the chestnut trees of Neuilly, my son Pierre sitting on my lap, and to feel his little fingers drumming their tattoo on the back of my hand.

I had a dream: I shall one day speak and walk again.

Part Two

"No one is obliged to deal with
the impossible."
— Stéphane Vigand

For Capucine, Juliette, and Pierre

Flashback

THERE IS A PHOTOGRAPH TAKEN JUST BEFORE the accident that shows a couple and their two small girls. We are in front of our country house in the Allier, where we go frequently on weekends and spend our vacations. Philippe comes from this region in central France, one we both love.

In the photograph, Philippe is thirty-three and I am twenty-eight. We had been married since September 10, 1982. Our decision to get married came four months after we met at a friend's house at Christmas, a quick decision but not an unconsidered one: We had fallen in love with each other.

Dynamic, tireless, demanding, possessed of a sense of modesty, willful — Philippe was a man of insatiable wants rather than ambitions. And he had a quality that is all too rare: passion. In his case, it was a boundless passion for animals, the woods, and above all for forestry, a calling he would have pursued if it had been a trifle more remunerative.

We spent the first year of our marriage in the United States. I had lived there before and liked the country. Philippe was less enthusiastic than I, but our year there was a happy one. And so were the years that followed, made up as they were of lightheartedness, of pleasure, of parties with friends, of weekends in our beloved Bourbonnais region and elsewhere, of all the things you take as they come and that end by seeming totally natural. Our life was a whirlwind, always in motion, and suited the two of us perfectly.

The births of our daughters Capucine, in October 1985, and of Juliette, in May 1989, hardly slowed the pace of our life. Imperceptibly, we were becoming settled. Philippe was controller at the French publishing firm Hachette; I was director of an advertising agency. His job was to anticipate, make forecasts, provide timely notice; mine was to work hard under tight deadlines. Each of us had found a kind of work that suited our temperaments. Our differences in character sometimes led to spats, but they were never over anything serious. Philippe, who I referred to as "Philou" in our more tender moments, would find himself addressed at those tenser times as "Vigand." But it never went much beyond that. We loved each other and were happy. Philippe was taking on new responsibilities at work, as well as devoting more time to stag hunting and golf — another of his passions — while I was carrying a full head of sail, with the wind at my heels. I was just starting to enjoy myself in my professional life. I was earning a good living and, like any serious advertising director, I was completely stressed out, fighting to meet deadlines.

For the summer holidays in 1990, we had made big plans. Philippe and I would spend a week in Tunisia, just the two of us, after which we would take the girls to the Basque country in the south of France, where we had rented a house. It was the first time we would be spending our vacation anywhere but at our country house.

Click.

I don't like looking at this snapshot. But without it and all it represents, nothing of what followed could ever have happened.

The Break with the Past

O*N JULY 4, 1990, SCARCELY FIFTEEN MINUTES* after I had arrived at the office, the telephone rang. It was a waiter at a café telling me that my husband had become indisposed in the street and that he had just been taken away in an ambulance. I rushed to the Neuilly Hospital, worried but not in any panic. In the car, I remembered that a month earlier, when we had finally managed to arrange a weekend for ourselves in the country without the girls, Philippe had come down with a terrific migraine, far worse than any he had known before. For three hours, from five in the morning until eight, I had scoured the neighboring villages for a doctor to try and relieve his pain. Once the migraine was gone, Philippe had refused to go to his doctor for any kind of checkup.

In the emergency room, I was made to wait for more than half an hour. An eternity. I fished a book from my bag and tried to read, until finally an intern arrived to tell me that Philippe was suffering from a severe headache. Reassuring as this news was, the diagnosis seemed in odd contrast with the nurses I could see racing back and forth at the end of the hallway. In his room, when I was finally allowed to enter it, there were five people bustling around him as he lay on his side, vomiting continuously, with a look on his face that I had never seen before. He could still speak and managed to describe his strange spell, then asked me to call a friend of ours who is a surgeon. This friend, who was in the middle of an operation, was kind enough to take my call. He told me to insist on having Philippe undergo an MRI scan as soon as possible.

We sped off in an ambulance to a hospital in Saint-Cloud. Philippe, lying on a stretcher, would open his eyes from time to time to say something sweet. He was also thinking out loud about what was happening to him, which he couldn't understand. Nor could I, but then I wasn't trying all that hard to understand: I had no reason not to believe the doctors. Magnetic resonance imagers, which were still rare at the time, provided a high-performance diagnostic test, and the results could be entirely trusted. Philippe's scan showed no abnormalities. There was therefore absolutely no reason to panic, even if the disturbing reality in front of me tended to contradict the doctors' reassurances.

At the time, I had no direct knowledge of doctors or hospitals. I had never had an operation, a broken arm, nothing. My only contact with the medical world had been during my two pregnancies. Now all I could do was give my blind faith to those who were poring over his case and had been by his bed since morning.

When we returned to Neuilly Hospital, they gave Philippe another examination. This one showed that there was a deficit on the left side, I was told. What does that mean, "a deficit on the left side"? I wanted to know. No one could tell me. Either they did not know or they didn't want to tell me. In any case, it made no difference: There was nothing more they could do.

At that point, perhaps more conscious than I of the gravity of his condition, Philippe asked me not to leave him, to stay by his bedside overnight. I stole away for a half hour to grab a few things, call my mother to pick up Juliette at the nanny's and keep her for the night, then call my parents-in-law, who had Capucine with them on vacation at Noirmoutier on the Atlantic coast, to let them know that their son was in the hospital with what I described as "an indisposition."

During the night, things snowballed. Around

2:00 A.M., Philippe tried to get up to go to the bathroom but had trouble staying on his feet. I couldn't hold him up, I had nobody to help me, I was afraid to call anyone. I was scared, feeling the tide of panic rising in me. That was the last time I saw Philippe on his feet.

At 6:00 A.M., he no longer answered when I spoke to him. By now he could not move his right arm and was getting all worked up trying to make it budge by using his left arm, although the effort was clearly painful. Aside from his motionless arm, the rest of his body still seemed more or less functional.

At 9:00 A.M., the doctor had already decided to have him transferred. He was being sent to Lariboisière Hospital, in the intensive care unit for trauma cases. Why there? Because there was a free bed? Because the head of the department was a friend of the Neuilly doctor? I'll never know. With me sitting beside him, the ambulance crossed Paris at rocket speed. Philippe's eyes were closed, he was totally unconscious, but I was convinced that he could hear me. I was allowed to accompany him as far as the door of the intensive care unit, where I was turned back. There was nothing more for me to do there, though I could come back during visiting hours. There were two half-hour visiting periods during the day, one beginning at 1:00 P.M., the other at 8:00 P.M.

My father joined me at the hospital and, as ever

when the going got tough, proved extraordinarily efficient and supportive. For two hours he helped me sort out the morass of administrative paperwork. Then he took me to a café, where we picked at our food without much conviction, killing time before my first visit.

I was in for a terrible shock. My husband had been whole when I left him at 9:30 A.M., and now, less than four hours later, I came back to find him completely hooked up to a support system, with wires, tubes, and medical machines everywhere, his eyelids taped shut. I was stunned. Unable to say a word, I stared at the machine. There were no words I could think of to say. They would come later, along with a horrible familiarity. At that moment, I only wanted him to survive all this. And what it was, according to the director of the clinic, a woman doctor, was a coma, brought on by a vascular accident, though how serious an accident she didn't know.

It was only a few days later that she tentatively diagnosed *locked-in syndrome*. As this barbarous and unfamiliar expression meant nothing to me, she added other words to it that were just as incomprehensible and indefinite: injury to the spinal bulb, basilar occlusion. . . . But what was the spinal bulb? And what does basilar occlusion mean, in concrete terms?

It meant that Philippe would awake from his coma paralyzed, but to what extent she could not say. Still unable to find my voice, I listened to this diagnosis as though watching the blade of a guillotine fall. A nurse added that "with a little luck, Philippe would be able to move his little finger in a year." Since I knew she could not possibly be making a joke, I tried to imagine the reality she was describing. Impossible. I knew Philippe, and I knew that if anyone could come through, he would.

My Own Coma

OUR LIFE HAD EXPLODED INTO A THOUSAND PIECES, but little by little it stubbornly worked its way back out of the chaos. In some cases, people simply don't have time to ask themselves whether they are strong enough to withstand a violent shock. Dazed and bewildered but still on my feet, I dealt with the most urgent demands to go on with life and do everything in my power to make sure Philippe could follow me on what was suddenly shaping up to be a very hazardous undertaking.

For two months I went to the hospital twice a day. Bruno, a loyal friend, picked me up at the office at lunchtime, and on our way there we would gulp down a sandwich in the car, filling the time with small talk. We talked about Philippe a great deal, of course, but we also chatted about all the trivial little things that are part and parcel of life. Sometimes Bruno went with me into Philippe's room, sometimes he waited outside. In the evening someone else would spell him and assume the very special role of chauffeur, companion, and moral supporter.

Philippe's friends came through with flying colors: always there for me, efficient, warmhearted, knowing instinctively what needed to be done. Thanks to them, and without my ever having to ask, I was never alone. During the visiting hours at the hospital or in the evening there was always someone to suggest that we go out to dinner together or do something else in the evening — a movie, a play — that would keep me from sinking into some sort of solitary feeling of hopelessness and despair. For two months, these friends proved to me over and over that there still was life outside that glass-enclosed room, into which one entered disguised as an extraterrestrial.

Two months can be a very long time. What was I to say to this man I love who gave scarcely any sign he could hear me? How could I dispel my own fear and at the same time breathe life into this terrifying place where the living dead and the terrified living mingle? I talked to him about everything: the children, work, the rumor of war in the Gulf. But it was sometimes hard to find words and, when they no longer came, I would massage Philippe's feet, simply to stay in contact with him. This was the only part of his body that I could more or less reach without running the risk that an awkward gesture of mine might unplug some machine. After a month of this treatment, he had managed not to get bedsores and his feet were as soft as a baby's. All the corns and calluses he had accumulated in thirty-three years of walking had melted away. And with them everything that even faintly resembled life as we had known it. Our life.

In the trauma intensive care unit, with its victims of automobile accidents, bludgeonings, bruisings, and beatings, Philippe truly stood out. But that gave me little comfort. Each visit found me waiting alongside the other families for permission to enter the glass cages. More than once our waiting period, already uncomfortably long, was prolonged to an alarming degree. We could guess, although we never voiced our thoughts, that a new emergency had arisen, and that a few yards away one of our loved ones was going down for the last time. Silently looking at one another as though nothing were the matter, each of us must have been praying that the drama then unfolding would touch someone else — not us! A strange feeling. And a strange kind of hope, which was dependent on someone else's death!

One day when I was visiting Philippe, I heard unusual noises from the neighboring room — machines in overdrive, family panicking, staff at full bustle. Then nothing. There was a heavy silence and the window was covered with a sheet, signs that it was all over. How short was the road from coma to death!

The next day, the scene was played out all over again, but this time in our own room. Machines going haywire, beeping on all sides, and myself in rigid paralysis watching Philippe's pulse oscillate from maximum to minimum. The nurses made me leave. Fifteen minutes later they came to get me. "Everything's normal again," they said, with the matter-of-fact calm that comes from experience, even the worst.

The same scene happened again several days or weeks later. Philippe was experiencing what are called septic shocks, enzyme surges that paralyze the entire immune system. In these circumstances, apparently, the healthier an organism, the more sensitive it is to any microorganism. And Philippe had the bad luck to be in perfect health. An accomplished sportsman, well muscled and active, he took good health almost to the point of caricature — characteristics one would expect to insulate him from harm.

Twice we teetered on the brink of complete catastrophe. And both times, once my terror had passed, I felt as if Philippe had taken advantage of my being there to let me know that all was still moving and alive inside, though it had meant going to the threshold of death to get the message out.

Comas are never simple, but his was particularly

ridden with complications. Aside from the two inci-
dences of septic shock, there were also (in random
order) a pleural infection, respiratory difficulties that
led to a tracheotomy, and severe dehydration, aggra-
vated by a heat wave, which made Philippe look like
the victim of a crucifixion brought down from his
cross to lie in agony on his shroud. His body, so well-
muscled when it had entered the ward, was now
reduced by some sixty pounds, leaving only the mis-
shapen shadow of what it had been.

In the very early days, I would call intensive care
two or three times a night to make sure that everything
was all right, or relatively so. But eventually I realized
that it was better to get my sleep so I could be on my
feet the next day. Because there would always be a
tomorrow, I was certain of that, even if afterward . . .

Philippe had always reproached me for failing to
project my life forward, to look to the future. My talent for living one day at a time, doing things at the last
moment, had always exasperated him. But it was def-
initely my capacity for living in the present that saved
me during the first months after Philippe's accident. If,
like him, I had focused on what lay ahead, I would
probably have put a bullet through my brain.

Work kept me going. For one thing, we were in
the middle of our annual reports, always an incredibly
busy period, and I took the opportunity to hunker
down among my files, making it a point of honor to

finish my reports on time. But my lunch hour often broke my concentration and sapped me of my good intentions. I would get back to the office in a panic around 3:00 P.M. thinking that Philippe was about to die, or that I was about to get an urgent call, or that I would go back there in the evening to find a sheet over the window and the cubicle empty.

At my ad agency I had a number of extraordinary friends, a real support system, ready to help, encourage, lend a helping hand. Philippe's accident had forged a wonderful solidarity among our friends and acquaintances, and their generosity, far greater than I could ever have imagined, was in large part responsible for keeping my head above water. What would I have done, and what would we have become, without our friends? Without my parents, who looked after our children, and have been indispensable adjuncts in raising them ever since the accident? Without Véronique, freshly returned from her honeymoon, who left her new husband to come and sleep at our house? Without all those whom I would come to meet and who, at every step of this ordeal, would prove that love and friendship have no bounds? The whole nightmare will at least have had the virtue of provoking a surge of vital forces. This is much more than just a simple consolation.

Code and Communication

Philippe awoke from his coma just as he had slipped into it, that is, both very gently and very quickly. Little by little they unplugged the machines.

I was obviously both happy and relieved that the worst had not happened, which is not to say I was exactly jumping for joy. . . . Oddly, it was only when Philippe awoke that I began to realize the full extent of the damage. His body was wasted and lifeless, his face was deformed, asymmetrical. There was his impressive tracheotomy, which had to be cleaned several times a day with a long probe. A dysfunction of his sweat glands made him perspire so that he was constantly drenched in sweat. Not a gesture, not a word. The only real change from his comatose state was that the doctors had removed the tape that kept his eyelids shut. Now they blinked. I focused on his eyes; in those eyes I recognized him. They told me that he could hear me and understand me. But how could we talk to each other? "Hello there! It's me, do you recognize me? . . ." And then what? One blink for yes, two blinks for no. But it wasn't easy to tell the voluntary and the reflex blinks apart. And you had to learn to ask the right questions. You could say: "Would you like me to open the window? . . ." and to that he could respond with a "yes" or "no." But if you forgot yourself and went on to say: "Or would you like me to lower the blinds?" he had no way of responding. So we would proceed methodically. "Do you want me to open the window?" If the answer was yes, fine, we would stop right there. If it was no, we went on: "So do you want me to lower the shade?" If it was still no, then go one step further: "Shall we leave it the way it is?" These are called *closed* questions. I was the only person who was convinced that Philippe was responding to them. The medical staff looked at me with great pity: after all, if it made me feel any better . . .

A decade ago, 99.9 percent of physicians, even neurologists, had never heard of locked-in syndrome. And those who had heard about it had never seen it firsthand. In other words, if from their vague knowledge of the subject they could affirm that the brain was intact, their entire attitude showed that they were firmly convinced they were dealing with a case of mental impairment. At the Salpêtrière Hospital, to which Philippe had been transferred, the doctor didn't even take the trouble to say hello to him when he happened to venture into his room. He would speak to me as if Philippe were not even there, or at least as if he was incapable of either hearing or understanding. In fact, no one made the slightest effort to talk to him. This went on for a very long time.

Without ever telling me so directly, the entire hospital staff did its best to let me know that the condition was irreversible and that there was no need for me to spend so much energy on behalf of the poor devil. But despite everything, I refused to give up, constantly confronting their imprecise diagnoses, their embarrassed silences, the alarmist comments I could not help overhearing, all of which always managed to destroy me completely.

To try and find out what lay ahead of us, I wanted to see others with locked-in syndrome. From talking about it to everyone I knew, I did manage to meet two or three people who knew someone with the syndrome, but I was never given the names or addresses of these fellow-sufferers, nor any details about their physical recovery. At the time, I felt alone, frustrated, and unassisted in dealing with what seemed to me to be a conspiracy of silence. Looking back on it now, I am actually grateful for their silence, their failure to respond. If, back in August 1990, I had actually seen other locked-ins and realized what our prospects were of making real progress — in this case, no prospects at all, in the sense in which this might be normally understood — I suspect I never would have battled on. In a sense, the doctors were right to tell me there was little or no hope. You have to live with it and break it down little by little. But some changes don't happen overnight. You have to keep telling yourself, "Take one day at a time"; no miracles between now and tomorrow, only tiny, invisible steps that, laid end to end, will eventually add up to remarkable improvements. In my case, I clung to the hope that Philippe would one day talk again, once his tracheotomy had been removed. That one day he would also walk again, even if imperfectly. At the same time I knew nothing would ever be the same as it had been, but also perhaps wanting to put behind me a piece of life that had broken off, one it was painful to remember, I went through his clothes at home, taking advantage of his absence to throw away those I didn't like.

As the harsh reality gradually sank in, I gave away all Philippe's personal effects that would no longer be of any use to him, starting with his suits, which were such a basic part of a work life he would never take up again. Some of our friends are still wearing them. . . . The only thing I kept were his ties, as a kind of symbol. And the shoes, which Philippe now wears again, without ever worrying about having to get them resoled. I really must have hoped and believed that he would walk again.

Looking at his physical decline, I had trouble keeping up my morale. The doctors maintained their obstinate silence, and I sometimes wondered whether Philippe was truly there. Toward the end of August, I started asking myself whether all this would not have to stop. One question continued to obsess me: Under these circumstances, how would Philippe live, with no hope of making any progress? I remember talking about it one night with several of our friends. No answer. Even with all my instincts still telling me to fight, I was within a hair's breadth of giving up. The private certainties that had supported me till then were weakening, and as they went, my energy started to flag.

Then one night, at the stroke of 11:00 P.M., the telephone rang. It was Philippe Van Eeckhout, the hospital speech pathologist: "My dear lady, I saw your husband today. I have spoken with him and I can assure you of one thing: There is nothing wrong with his comprehension, any more than with yours or mine." The words I had been waiting for, hoping for, all these weeks!

If I was crazy to believe that Philippe's mind was intact, at least I was not the only one. There were two of us, and we were that much the stronger for it. This was not just an enormous relief, but it gave me the impetus I sorely needed to get going again. Because first there had been the coma to deal with, then the awakening. But what came after? Frightening reality, plus damning verdicts from the medical community, which I was trying to refute on the basis of Philippe's blinking eyelids. Van Eeckhout had just supplied me with a goal and defined an urgent need: to give Philippe a way to communicate.

We owe the idea of a code to my friend Véronique. But I owe its shape to my overwhelming urge to talk to my husband and to prove to all the skeptics that his brain was intact. In half an hour I concocted the grids of consonants and vowels that we still use today. A friend from the agency took care of the actual physical presentation: a large signboard, carefully lettered, underlined, framed, and coated in plastic (a necessary precaution because of my husband's drenching fits of coughing). Arriving at the hospital, I brandished our signboard triumphantly under Philippe's nose.

For anyone willing to make the effort, it only takes a few days to learn the code. But undeniably it demands certain mental gymnastics and a great deal of concentration. Translating Philippe takes one's undivided attention, and even the slightest distraction is fatal. To indulge in some other activity, be it as mundane and mechanical as peeling potatoes, while "listening" to him, is out of the question. When he "speaks," you have to focus totally on his eyelids to decipher each letter and try to make out the sentence. For all its qualities, the code has no apostrophe, no cedilla, no accents, no space between words — all of which tends to make deciphering difficult, especially when voluntary blinks are interrupted by reflex blinks, a telephone call, or a child's interruption. How many times have I almost lost my mind at having to start a sentence all over again because of an interruption of one kind or another? Words with a cedilla are particularly treacherous, cropping up when I least expect them.

Speaking with the code is a long, laborious task. Whereas it takes me about three seconds to say, "Would you hand me the book that Emmanuel left on the table?" it also takes Philippe three seconds to think it but a good five minutes to make himself understood! To save time, the temptation is to finish Philippe's sentences with your own words, telling yourself that the substitution is unimportant, since the main thing is to understand what he means. But like each of us, Philippe needs *his* words, without which no real communication is possible. Or else he would have to limit himself to certain basic signals: for example, spelling out the word H-E-A-D, meaning that he needs someone to reposition his head, or H-A-N-D, to let us know that his hand has slipped from his armrest. As dialogue, these fall a bit short.

You have to accept the fact that any conversation worthy of the name has to take place over time, and in a setting of calm. Therefore, the best time for Philippe and me to talk is in the evening, after 9:00 P.M., when, with his aide-de-camp gone for the day and the children in bed, we are finally alone. Unfortunately for Philippe, however, this is also the time when, exhausted by a long and busy day, I would like nothing more than to plunk myself down in front of the television set or read a good book. By midnight, I need matchsticks to prop my eyes open, and I sometimes have to interrupt him: "This is the last sentence, then I'm stopping. . . ." You might think that all I have to do is avert my gaze from Philippe's eyelids, but that would be to grossly underestimate all the means he has at his disposal to keep me from sleeping and convince me to go on interpreting him — simply the grinding of his teeth alone would awake the deaf! And for so long now I have wanted him to speak like anyone else, and say (almost) everything that passes through his head, important things but also all sorts of small talk. I humbly confess that there are some nights I wish he would restrict himself to important things, but I also know that communication — dialogue and under-standing — are made up of a thousand little things that we need to share. So I go on interpreting him and invariably get annoyed. But we do manage to under-stand each other; in fact, I sometimes wonder whether we don't talk to each other a great deal more than most couples do.

For a long time I was Philippe's only translator and interpreter. Some people, no doubt hoping he would one day speak again, refused to learn the code and were quite happy to monologue and receive an occasional eye blink by way of response. The rest of the time they would turn to me for help, as if to remind me I was shirking duties or just plain lazy, whereas all I had in mind was to get a bit of rest. I especially remember one incident that occurred roughly a year after the accident. It was summer; we were staying at our country house in Allier and would often stop by my parents-in-law's, who lived nearby, to use their swimming pool. To say that they were having trouble accepting what had happened to their son would be a gross understatement. Even after a year, still pained and confused, overwhelmed by the enormity of the situation, they could not bring themselves to believe that Philippe was mentally intact or talk to him "normally," as you would to any thirty-three-year-old man, without an intermediary. That summer, as soon as I was in the pool Philippe would try to say something and I would be called on to come help, dropping everything to tell them what their darling son was saying. Until one day I finally blew up: I had the right, I believed, to a few minutes' respite, and I thought it might be desirable, if not indispensable, for my father-

and mother-in-law to make an effort to learn the code, which we had been using for almost a year now!

It was not my only outburst. I also lashed out at some of our more refractory friends for hoping too hard that Philippe would regain his speech. And there were others to whom I gave hell for refusing to look him in the eye or who avoided his gaze because they felt uncomfortable.

Since then, all of them have more than made up for their behavior. In fact, I have the feeling that Philippe has never been in such close touch with his father. Among his friends, there are at least a dozen who are able to use the code with consummate ease. This allows for real relationships, without the intervention of any third party, and makes dinners with our friends much easier. To make himself understood and speak up in the midst of a yammering group of eight or ten, Philippe puts on what I call his "donkey act": He nods his head like a yo-yo until we notice him. At which all eyes turn immediately in his direction, and each person observes a momentary, almost reverent, silence. Quite often, Philippe's sentence relates to something said five minutes earlier, and by now forgotten by everyone but him, which adds another layer of difficulty to the challenge of understanding him.

Always speaking with a delay, and having endlessly to depend on an interpreter who may or may not grasp what you're saying, has to be a constant source of frustration for him. But it should be recognized that, for all its imperfections, the code is a kind of miracle in its own right. So we all make do with it, including me. For Philippe to be confined to a wheelchair is something I can accept. But I still cannot get used to the fact that he doesn't talk. For a long time the sound of his voice continued to resonate within me. Today I have forgotten it. And when the children settle in to watch the home videos we made before the accident occurred, I steal quietly away so that I don't have to hear his voice.

Luckily, we have the computer. It helps make up for many of the code's shortcomings and reduces its frustrations. Through the written word much more than the chopped-up utterances of the code, I find the Philippe I once knew. He was never much given to idle chatter or going on at great lengths conversationally, but his accident and the need to go straight to the point have made him a reductionist's reductionist. To hell with flourishes and circumlocutions! Long live concision!

The sweet nothings uttered in a moment of transport can be forgotten, and the threats, recriminations, and insults tossed back and forth at one another in a moment of anger can, if necessary, be forgiven. But printed on paper, they assume a whole other weight and resonance. It is said that the written word survives. . . . But I have learned to give the lie to this truism. At first I religiously preserved every scrap of paper that carried the sacred word, as if I were amassing evidence. Little by little, for lack of space (four or five messages a day for nine-plus years begin to constitute a library) and to lighten my load, I began to make a selection, keeping only the pearls. Love notes, as beautiful as those Philippe wrote me during our courtship, and just as seductive; funny notes and furious notes; notes that were full of spite and vengeance, and which I often read "cold" because they had been composed after, say, some argument we had had in the morning and I would find them only upon returning home in the evening. My husband could have had them thrown away by his aide-de-camp, Emmanuel, in the course of the day, but when he has something to tell me, he wants me to hear it, even several hours later.

To be sure, I'm not the only one who sees such notes. The children, as well as our extended family and friends, have, when they arrive at the house, all acquired the habit of dipping a hand in the mailbox (a sack hung from the arm of his wheelchair) to see if they have any messages. Everybody tries to curb his or her curiosity about the messages destined for others. In any case, thanks to the computer, Philippe has recovered his power of speech. Impossible now for us to pretend we don't hear his silent words.

From Challenge to Challenge

GETTING ORGANIZED, MAKING Philippe more comfortable, doing my best to make sure he regains as much independence as possible despite his disability: in short, trying to have our life take on some semblance of normality — for a long time these were my only goals. Every objective on which I set my (our) sights seemed enough of a challenge to motivate me not to stop. I constantly had to move forward, even if it meant going a bit overboard, to the point where others couldn't figure out what I was doing and I myself became exhausted. Far from fulfilling me, far from satisfying even temporarily my deep-seated need to move mountains, every victory — or every step that seemed to spell progress — simply served as a springboard for other possibilities.

★　　　★　　　★

My first challenge: to arrange for Philippe's weekend stays at home while he was still a patient at Garches. The logistics for this perilous and athletic adventure were worthy of a major battle. To ensure that Philippe would enjoy a reasonable level of comfort during his "leaves," the hospital supply office had offered me an entire battery of barbaric equipment: a motorized bed, a lift. . . . I could not bring myself to accept the first, because the apartment was too small for an additional bed. When Philippe came home he would sleep with me in *our* bed, one we had bought just before the accident. It was wide, spacious . . . and practically at floor level. Sorry, on this point I refused to yield. The day before Philippe's first visit home, I called on a friend for help, and together we raised the bed to the right height with the help of eight assorted foreign-language dictionaries, three telephone books, and a few other carefully chosen tomes. As for the lift, there was so little space in which to move it around that we used it only once. As a result, transfers from the bed to the wheelchair, and from the wheelchair to the bed, were made using the strong arms of our volunteers . . . to the detriment of their backs. But at least the apartment had not been turned into a hospital.

It took a number of skillful maneuvers to reach this little nest of ours, which I took pains to keep cozy. The building's elevator was too narrow for the wheelchair, so Philippe had to be transferred onto a regular chair while the ambulance team took his wheelchair up the stairs. During these weekends we were able to make outings, thanks to the invaluable help of the couple Tino and Hilda, who managed the building. Without our ever having to ask them, Tino would lend us a hand lifting and carrying Philippe, while Hilda would look after the girls for whatever time it took us to go up or down. They were kind, attentive, indispensable, ready at a moment's notice to extricate me from whatever problems had arisen in the course of the day. Even today, if I am ever in a bind I know I can call on them day or night and they will be there.

Philippe's transportation between Garches and home quickly became another problem that had to be dealt with immediately. We were entitled to an ambulance and medics, but this arrangement, we knew, could not last forever. If we wanted to be self-sufficient we would need a car — and not just any car! It would have to be roomy enough to contain a wheelchair; a car customized so that Philippe could be held securely in place throughout the trip; thus we would not need to lift him in and out and find sophisticated restraints to keep his head from wobbling back and forth. We already owned a van, a Renault Espace; all we needed to do was to fit it out. The only possible solution was to install a hoist at the back that could raise and lower the wheelchair without ejecting its occupant.

The hoist was installed in the spring of 1991, and

the system allowed us to advance several giant steps along the path toward independence, even if every trip still had elements of a high-risk adventure: Philippe could still not support his head at the time, and every bump made him so seasick he was likely to throw up. Since then, things have improved, and I have learned to drive with one eye focused on the rearview mirror, so that I can decode Philippe's expression and check the movements of his head. If he gurgles inordinately or suddenly throws up, the children take it upon themselves as a matter of course to break out the paper towels.

The prospect of spending the summer vacation at our country house raised for the first time a crucial question: where to put Philippe? I had no intention of keeping him out of our bedroom, but I also couldn't see myself climbing the spiral staircase leading up to it carrying him in my arms. Sometimes, I do acknowledge my own limitations. A brilliant suggestion from my father solved the problem: We had a barn next to our house renovated, which involved a fair amount of construction and some quasi–Hollywood style furnishings, among them a gigantic bathtub, comfortable for a disabled person and utterly luxurious for the children. Four or five can fit in it together, and often the children amuse themselves for hours in this improvised swimming pool, the envy of their playmates.

I probably should have taken advantage of our first vacation together to get some rest, but my fighting spirit willed otherwise. I had convinced myself that Philippe would one day eat again. At the time he was force-fed, rather than nourished, through a gastric tube connected to the duodenum, through which a whitish liquid, which gave Philippe a pasty complexion and would have ruined anyone's appetite, was introduced. Aside from the fact that every additional piece of equipment made it harder to overlook Philippe's disability, it seemed to me that he was entitled to at least a few pleasures, in particular those of eating tasty food that would satisfy his taste buds.

However, I knew this pleasure might prove costly. Ever since his accident, Philippe had had great trouble swallowing and had lost the reflex that automatically sends food into the esophagus. The result: Our tasty little dishes could well end up in his lungs, the consequences of which we did not even want to contemplate.

Philippe's gourmandise, coupled with his natural desire to enjoy the few pleasures still available to him, induced him to take up the challenge. The task, however, proved far more difficult than I had thought, but seconded by the faithful Madeleine, a peerless cook, I managed, after countless attempts, to have him swallow well-blended foods. This endless and laborious operation took us two months of concerted effort and never less than five hours a day: an hour at breakfast, two at lunch, and two more at dinner. There were failures and regurgitations, followed by miles of paper towel, feelings of great impatience, and an urge to chuck the whole thing, but we finally succeeded.

Today Philippe can eat like anyone else, even though in what we call the "pureed-delayed" mode. Mealtimes still provide hazardous moments, with many small catastrophes, due to food that is too hot, puree that is too thick or, most commonly, things going down the wrong way. After long and heart-rending discussions, we have given up on family dinners, during which I am supposed to serve the meal, channel and control the children's irrepressible energy, and interpret their father's comments. He takes his meals alone, assisted by an aide-de-camp, but later joins us at table, where no one would think of usurping his place. And when we have dinner at a friend's house, our hosts never forget to prepare doggie bags so that Philippe can verify whether the dinner, ground up in the blender the next day, was as good as we claimed.

These same friends have contributed in large measure to our meeting a further challenge I had set myself when Philippe returned home: to resume a normal social life. Without their help, more than one dinner would have ended abruptly with us stuck on the sidewalk because an elevator was too small or out of service. But there are always strong arms to pick Philippe up on one side and the wheelchair on the other and hoist the package to our destination. A few hours later, the same strong arms, despite (or thanks to) a few glasses of alcohol consumed in the meantime, perform the entire operation in reverse. Sometimes there are bumps, slips, or grazed extremities, and always a great deal of hearty laughter. When our friends live somewhere truly inaccessible, the dinner is held at our house, but we come as guests!

On another front, we have finally figured a way to go the movies unassisted — a daring feat when you consider the number of steps up or down one has to take to penetrate into dark theaters. As luck would have it, there are two movie houses not far from our house that are wheelchair accessible. This is nothing short of a miracle in a country where the handicapped are to all intents and purposes asked to spend their cloistered lives at home, without ever going out. Nevertheless, pleasure has to be earned, and for us to see even the worst lemon, major maneuvers are required. First of all, there is the problem of parking. After circling a heavily trafficked square no fewer than three times, we finally find *the* ideal spot, where we will have enough room to activate the hoist and lower the wheelchair, all of which does not prevent us from getting a parking ticket, despite the impressive blue "major disability" sticker prominently displayed on the windshield. Then we enter the movie theater . . . by the exit! Each time we do, I engage in a protracted wrestling match with several sets of heavy two-sided fire doors. With one hand I press the bar to open one side of the door, blocking it open with my foot or buttocks while holding on to the wheelchair, my body arched against it, then press on the bar with my other hand to release the second side of the door. Oof! Then I have to start all over again with the second set of doors, before we can make our grand entrance into the theater, which I assure you never goes unnoticed. Once inside, we have to confront the compassionate, or terrified, looks of the moviegoers and, more often than not, the misplaced zeal of a neophyte usherette who instructs me in no uncertain terms to move Philippe onto one of the vacant theater seats. ("You can't sit in the aisle, you know!") To convince her that the idea is unworkable, my husband starts to spit and cough, which irritates me to no end but usually convinces the usher not to insist any further. Whatever protests it may provoke, the wheelchair stays parked next to the fire exit. At least Philippe will be at the head of the line if ever there is a fire. One has to keep looking at the positive side of things! When the film is good, I've managed to put the whole problem behind me by the time the lights come on again two hours later. When it's bad, I am willing to go through the ordeal all over again, but only on the condition that they say "pretty please!"

My penchant for taking up challenges has sometimes led to misunderstandings and incomprehension. The computer is one good example. After using it on a daily basis for several years, Philippe was perfectly satisfied with it. I wasn't. The machine functioned like a simple typewriter, and I deplored the fact that it was not equipped with a full word processor capable of scrolling backward, cutting, pasting, and all the other little amenities of computer technology. Philippe didn't see the point of it, but I was as usual stubborn, and a few months later the new word processor was in place. The only glitch was that, as it was being installed, the thing imploded and Philippe was left without any computer at all for two long months, unable to communicate except via the old eye-blink code. Isn't there an old expression that says the best is the enemy of the good? Rightly so, Philippe blamed the whole problem on my stubbornness. He may have forgiven me by now, since that same word processor, once repaired, enabled him to write this book!

As I faced one challenge after the other, Philippe must often have thought I wasn't paying enough attention to him, but in fact all I was doing was thinking of us both, which meant planning ahead. This constant pre-occupation with the future now seems in retrospect to me to have been a necessary evil: By setting practical goals for myself, I kept my mind from wandering off into the realm of sterile questions and useless lamentations.

Have we gone as far as we could, done as much as was possible? Whether we have or not, it does seem to me that today there are fewer challenges to face, and I must confess I sometimes miss them. But I realize that it's pointless to want to succeed on all fronts. I'm aware of my limitations and know how to husband my energies. At present the greatest challenge, and perhaps the only one, is learning to hold out in the long run.

Don Quixote and the
Bureaucracy

*H*OW MANY TIMES HAVE I HAD THE FEELING that I was tilting at windmills and shouting in the desert? An indefatigable Don Quixote, unswayed by sarcasm and incomprehension, I knew that my battles were far from insignificant, and I threw myself into them wholeheartedly. It was not faith that saw me through, but my desire to see the man I love provided with a decent life. Even if the outcome sometimes did not live up to my expectations, some of the victories have rewarded me generously for my efforts.

Locked-in syndrome is so rare a disorder that its victim is automatically viewed as a strange creature. For

144

a long time some people considered Philippe mentally impaired. Despite all the evidence marshaled by medical science to demonstrate that Philippe's brain was as good as ever, few were willing to believe it. The first battle was to convince them of the clarity and intelligence of his mind. It was my duty to repeat over and over again to the doctors and nurses that it was their responsibility to talk to him, or at least treat him like a full-fledged human being, one more sensitive than most, a man with his own sufferings, desires, and needs. But how could they ever understand this when, straining under the weight of their own demanding workloads, they never had time to learn the eye-blink code?

Since Philippe could neither make any requests nor voice any complaints, I became his intermediary, and my relations with the hospital staff were often stormy, sometimes downright hostile. In all fairness, the situation I was facing did make me short-tempered and irritable (the word is not strong enough), and the hospital staff was terribly shorthanded. I had the feeling I had to fight for everything at every turn: to obtain a shade so Philippe would not melt from the burning sun that streamed in through his window; to keep the staff from chewing him out at night on the pretext that he was coughing too loudly; to point out that it was no use stealing his alarm clock or his radio from under his nose, since his sight was unimpaired; to ask them to brush his teeth, wash his hair, put him in his wheel-chair before I arrived; to put him to bed for the night in the proper way, with his shoulders to the right and his buttocks to the left (the only position he finds comfortable); to make sure they changed his sweat suit periodically, that they picked him up and put him down gently. . . . In a word, that they take decent care of him! When the doctors and the nurses finally started to get the picture, it would be time to send him to a new ward. And so I would have to start all over again at zero, explaining the full particulars of his case and the care he required.

But even before then, we faced an uphill battle to get Philippe admitted *anywhere*. No hospital wanted to take him, because he did not fit any of the standard categories. My greatest fear was that he would be sent to Berck, a hospital on the English Channel that was too far away from Paris. On balance, I even preferred Garches. At least it was nearby; the girls and I could get there easily, as could his friends. The first year Philippe had been kept on there grudgingly, but in the fall of 1991 I was informed that I would have to find a place for him somewhere else. Fortunately, our strokes of ill fate have always been accompanied by a modicum of luck. This time it took the form of Dr. Dizien, who was the idol of the disabled patients in another ward at Garches. Toward the end of the summer, my sister-in-law Pascale and I decided to pay him a call. Putting all our chips on the table, we went to the meeting wearing our shortest skirts and our most captivating smiles, but still found that, despite our drop-dead looks, we had to sell Philippe point by point, like any good advertising women. He now had a computer, he ate pureed food: in short, he was making real progress. Was it in repayment for our efforts that Dizien agreed to give Philippe a bed in his ward? It was another battle won, but there was no time to savor it. Now we had to brief a new set of nurses, speaking loudly and firmly enough to make our points, but knowing when to stop before our efforts became counterproductive. In taking care of Philippe, we were given to understand, the hospital was doing us a great favor. If I pushed too hard, they might just ask me to find a bed for him somewhere else.

Even with all our difficulties and crossed communications, due largely to the fact that Philippe's case is so rare and requires such special care, there have over the years been many health workers who turned out to be patient, good humored, self-sacrificing, kind, and well-intentioned, but there were also many others, I must say, who were often unequal to the task of dealing with an unusual disorder that did not fit any of the categories covered in their nursing school manuals.

A prime example of the latter type was the so-called expert who came to examine Philippe on his return home from the hospital. I was claiming that we had the right to physical therapy sessions at the proper fee, which Social Security was denying us. My entreaties escalated from phone calls to registered letters. When these met with polite refusals, I made an appeal, until I found myself in court requesting to have an expert appraisal of our case. The poor man detailed by the court to perform the appraisal, a general practitioner, acted out a scene worthy of *Candid Camera*. He planted himself in front of Philippe, grew annoyed when his questions elicited no answer, eventually agreed to have me act as Philippe's interpreter, then tested his reflexes with a small hammer (totally stupid to anyone who understands the slightest thing about locked-in syndrome!), and then asked Philippe to stand up! Obtaining no response, he declared that, as he had thought, Philippe had no need of so-called heavy physical therapy and we should be satisfied with the Social Security fees already allotted us. I thought I was going to faint; it took me three days to recover, but the battle goes on. What with the Social Security Administration (SSA), the Family Allocation Fund (FAF), and other acronym-prone organizations, I have no time to grow bored. We have several major, and apparently interminable, lawsuits in progress.

The laws, not designed with our case in mind, as well as a whole host of others, have led to more than one aberration. When, after Pierre's birth, I resumed my professional activities, I fully expected to receive child-care support. Alas! France boasts of the assistance it offers families with three children in the form of child-care help, but it does so only on the condition that both parents work. Clearly not our case. Philippe, who receives a pension but not a wage, was therefore free (they informed us) to take care of his son! If we wanted a nanny, that was our problem! But I was right not to throw in the sponge — finally, the court ruled in our favor!

You have to fight for everything you want. In the eyes of the government, the bare minimum is considered ostentatious luxury. As the president of the French Association of Paralyzed People once humorously remarked: "Only the rich can afford to be quadriplegic." How right he is! The support we receive from our families, always forthcoming, has preserved us from want and anxiety, but how many people are fighting just to provide themselves with a decent wheelchair? If only Philippe's story might serve to get a few things moving in the right direction . . .

What vast amounts of time and energy I have wasted on these administrative hassles, so much so that I have become the crown queen of paperwork! I who hated paperwork with a passion am now familiar with every form and questionnaire of every department in all the medical centers. Not to mention hospital admission forms, work contracts, wage slips, Social Security forms, letters of dismissal . . . among so many others. On a recent curriculum vitae, under the heading "professional experience," I wrote: "Head of a family business." Certificates upon request.

Pierre

*H*OW *DO YOU CONCEIVE A CHILD* when your partner
has locked-in syndrome? Bad-mouthers and doubting
Thomases notwithstanding, you do it the same as anyone else would, during a night of love.

The difference is that I was not at all planning to
have another child. In our "first" life, we had always
theorized that it would be nice to have three children,
but our first life was already far behind us. I was
experiencing "physiological and cyclical dysrhyth-
mia," most likely due to the psychological shock of
Philippe's accident, and I thought it would protect me.
But on my return from a week's vacation the fact
dawned on me ineluctably: I was pregnant. And
incredulous. When an ultrasound confirmed it, I tried
to put some order into my thoughts by pouring myself

a gin and tonic. I was happy, but I had no intention of sharing the news with anyone else — there were already so many things I had to explain.

The truth is, I had built a hard shell for myself as insulation against the hospital smells, its bureaucratic battles, my own anguish, and all the things that eat away at and destroy you, and with time the shell had grown thicker and thicker. A baby is a little ball of tenderness, a feeling I had completely lost, though I very much wanted to allow it to flower again. The first person I let in on the secret was Pascale. I took my time breaking the news to Philippe. A few weeks later, arriving at his room in Garches, I opened the envelope and spread out the ultrasound pictures in front of him. The joy he felt literally brought him out of his wheelchair. When I saw his reaction, I knew that we were doing the right thing and that our child would have a real father.

That day, by common consent, we decided to wait until Christmas to make the announcement public.

On Christmas night 1991, we had gathered our two families around us at our country house, and, in the middle of dinner, I asked everyone to be silent because Philippe had something to tell them. I designated my father-in-law to play the part of interpreter. Assuming his responsibilities with an air of seriousness and evident goodwill, he began spelling the message out: W-E-A-R-E-E-X-P-E-C-T-I-N-G-A-T . . .

There he stopped, giving the signal for the now-traditional guessing game to start. "A train . . ." my mother suggested nervously, making Philippe, Pascale, and me howl with laughter. As for my father-in-law, he was clearly stumped, and since no one wanted, or was able, to come up with the rest, I came to his rescue, starting the sentence from the top: "We are expecting a third child."

Surprise, embarrassment, disbelief: The reactions that followed our announcement reflected all three of the above. Mother was stunned, Father disconcerted, my two brothers in stitches. . . . After a moment of stupefaction, my father-in-law came forward to embrace Philippe and tell him, with tears in his eyes and his voice, how happy he was to know that a new life was forming. My mother-in-law, who had remained oddly silent during the entire scene, rose from the table, took her coat, and left the room. We thought she had gone to get the presents for the adults' traditional exchange of Christmas gifts, but she never came back. . . .

No present. Fine. We already had ours: a child. We got the best of the bargain. Everyone needed time to digest the surprise we had sprung on them.

Our parents' reactions did not keep us from broadcasting the news to a wider circle. A week later, we organized a New Year's Eve party for our friends, where we repeated the little scene we had played at

Christmas. This time there were two notable differences: I had no need to finish Philippe's sentence and no one was frozen in astonishment. The reactions we received were spontaneous and warm, expressing friendship and emotion, letting us know that our friends considered Philippe and me a normal couple.

My pregnancy at least gave all the naysayers, male and female, a chance to criticize to their heart's content! Most of them thought it was crazy to have a child with a disabled mate. Some saw me as a reincarnation of the Virgin, still others preferred to see me as representing the miracle of in vitro fertilization. Still others took great pleasure in viewing me as a man-eater and waited impatiently for the child to be born so that the game of guessing who the *real* father was could begin.

Although I have a pretty thick skin and a fair share of self-confidence, these insinuations hurt me enormously. But it was far from my first boo-boo. And the nasty gossip in no way lessened the pleasure of expecting a child. Philippe's dream was to have three girls, four women in all, probably imagining himself as a sultan reigning over his harem. I wanted a boy, and it was now or never — I knew that it would be my last venture into the domain of parenthood.

Our son was born on June 30, 1992 — almost two years to the day from Philippe's accident — in a clinic at Montluçon in the Allier. A relatively small baby at six pounds thirteen ounces, he had the blue eyes of his maternal grandfather, which swept away any last reservations and left everyone reconciled. We named him Pierre. Having both the sense of *rock* and of *Peter*, the name seemed not only to fit but necessary, a symbol of rebuilding a new and solid life.

Albeit smaller in frame than either of his two sisters, Pierre has always been endowed with a high energy level. Nonetheless, at several stages of his development I noted that he seemed visibly slow for his age. An active and wiggly baby, he would become the quietest little boy when he was put into his stroller, hardly twitching his nose. I was intrigued by his immobility, and it took me a long time to discover where it came from: Ever since he was born, I had been in the habit of taking him on walks by plunking him down on his father's lap. While I can push either a wheelchair or a stroller, I have never been clever or talented enough to handle both at once. In order not to slide off, Pierre had been forced to stay perfectly still. Once he was put back in his stroller, imitating his father, he behaved in a like manner. Since then I have noticed more than once that no sooner is a child put on Philippe's lap than he sits perfectly still, not even moving a finger.

When Pierre was seven months old he still could not sit up. As it is my nature not to notice things that bother me, I didn't pay too much attention to it. All this changed one day when I was watching a television program with Caroline Eliacheff, a child psychiatrist. Explicitly, and with the help of many examples, she was explaining how children could be cured of a number of different symptoms simply by talking to them about their parents' stories and the choices and circumstances that had led to their present lives. This hit me like a ton of bricks. Completely absorbed as I had been in the day-to-day struggle just to keep afloat, I had never taken the time to tell Pierre what had happened to his father. The very next day, using the words that came to mind on the spur of the moment, I told him the whole story and encouraged him not to take his father as a role model in every last detail. For instance, I told him, he had the right to sit up and to squirm around in his stroller if he felt like it. Two days later Pierre was sitting up by himself.

Roughly a year later there was another hitch in his development. Pierre, now eighteen months old, was still not walking. In fact, he seemingly was not even making an effort to stand up. At around that same time, I was putting our library in order when I came across a book by Caroline Eliacheff that I had bought after hearing her television program. This time I had no need to reread it. I took my son aside for a heart-to-heart talk, and told him that his father was most anxious to see him walk like all the other little children. A few days later, if it wasn't the very next day, Pierre was not only walking but running around like a little trooper.

At the age of three, Pierre again seemed blocked in his development. He babbled, as babies and toddlers do, but didn't speak a single word. This time it was some friends who helped me understand. "Your son is funny, he talks like his father, by batting his eyelashes," they said one night as they came out of the children's bedroom after kissing them goodnight. I hadn't even noticed. Being the little man that he is, again taking his father as role model, Pierre was imitating his father, speaking only by blinking his eyelids. I wasted not a minute to explain to him that Philippe would talk like everyone else if he could, and that we were all of us anxious to hear the sound of his little voice. In a matter of a few weeks, Pierre started talking with astonishing facility, avoiding most of the faults that children make when they first begin to talk.

Detractors of psychoanalysis can make of this whatever they like.

I am now firmly convinced of the importance of saying things and of repeating them as often as necessary. Some years ago, when he was four, Pierre asked me: "When Dad's hole is stopped up, will he be able to walk again?" Once again, I had to explain what had happened and what we could reasonably hope for. Something understood at one moment must be reexplained at every succeeding stage of development in words appropriate to that stage. For one thing, Pierre needs to be able to answer all the questions his little playmates must surely ask him when Philippe goes to pick him up at school. One day a little girl, the daughter of a friend of ours, who was used to coming to the house but had just reached the age where children start to notice things, refused to go near Philippe. Pierre took her by the hand, and as they walked away I heard his version of the story: "You know, it happened a long time ago. Dad fell down in the street and a pebble hit him on the head so he can't walk anymore. But it doesn't matter, he can roll in his wheelchair."

The hardest thing, really, was to get Pierre to kiss Philippe. For a long time he stubbornly refused, doubtless waiting for his father to set the example so he could follow. But if teaching him to kiss was a long, slow process, Pierre has more than made up for it since.

Children Like Any Others

OUR THREE CHILDREN LOVE TO PORE OVER the family photo albums, which they are prone to do for hours on end. I watch them from afar, reluctant to look at these now-painful images again.

Unlike their brother, Capucine and Juliette are no doubt searching for their father as they once knew him, standing, on his own two feet, though Juliette has no conscious memory of it and talks about the time when "Dad was a normal man." Pierre looks with a certain curiosity at this man he never knew, who bears little resemblance to his father.

At the time of Philippe's accident, the two eldest children reacted in very different ways. During the first two months, caught up in the ongoing emergency, I was forced to neglect them, or at least leave them on the sidelines as the drama unfolded. Unaware of what the future might hold, I didn't know what to tell them, and my courage failed me. It was perhaps also a way of protecting them. It happened during summer vacation period, and both girls were at my parents' house. I put off having to make explanations that would not only be upsetting and painful to me but traumatic to them.

I saw Capucine for the first time about ten days after the accident. She told me all about her holiday in Brittany, the exploits of her cousins, and what had happened at the beach. Then, as though suddenly noticing that Philippe was not around, she asked me if her dad was still in bed because of his headache. Yes, he was still in bed. . . . What was the point of saying anything more?

But when the school year started in September, when the normal rhythm of our life resumed, and Philippe's absence from the daily round had to be confronted, with its destabilizing effect on the family, Capucine came close to falling apart, obviously consumed with pain and rage. Her nerves were frayed to the breaking point; she raised her voice at everything and nothing, as if to deny the unimaginable truth. Her father's accident had hit her very, very hard. Ever since she was a babe in arms, she had always gravitated toward him, and they got along extremely well. With her, Philippe loosened up and let himself express his full tenderness. Now, from one day to the next, her world had collapsed.

The first visit to Garches, on her fifth birthday, was a nightmare. I decided to take her to a psychoanalyst to help her, as far as was possible, accept the unacceptable.

Juliette was just the opposite. Perhaps protected by the happy-go-lucky outlook of a fourteen-month-old, she continued at any rate to be what she had always been, a little ball of energy and fun. Seeing her leap up and wrap her arms around my neck, or hearing her burst out laughing, has helped me hold on more than anything. On the first visit to Garches with her sister, it was heartwarming to see how spontaneously she jumped onto her father's bed, without the slightest hesitation, as though it were nothing at all, as though he had always been like that, lying motionless on his back. What she did, which in ordinary times I would have taken as completely ordinary, in and of itself had the power to outline the continuity of our life.

It is thanks in large part to Juliette that I never asked myself whether I had the right to subject my children to this kind of life. And it is thanks to our loyal friends, Antoine and another Philippe, alias Chewchew, who acted as surrogate fathers during the girls' real father's hospital stay, that their lives retained some degree of equilibrium in the turbulent tide that washed over us. My children's lives, like anyone else's, consist of joys and pleasures, but also of bumps and hurts, of major metaphysical discussions, and of silences freighted with grief.

Is this their way of protecting me? They never complain in my presence, never tell me of the taunts and mean words or deeds that most certainly come their way regularly, both at school and elsewhere. I always learn of these in roundabout ways.

Although during the early months after the accident Juliette was full of laughter, she pays for it now by sometimes breaking down. She becomes blocked, shuts herself away, and turns in on herself until, all of a sudden, she overcomes her bouts of anguish and once again her laughter rings out, contagious and irresistible. When she was little, she was fascinated by the story of Sleeping Beauty and watched the video over and over again. Then one day she asked me: "Tell me, Mama, can Sleeping Beauty move her arms and her legs?" Later, with a wisdom beyond her years, she announced that she preferred "to have a daddy who is disabled than a daddy who is dead."

When she was ten, Capucine asked if she could go away to boarding school. It may well have been that the situation was too difficult to deal with, or it may have been that she and I are too much alike, and sparks often fly when our personalities come into contact

with each other. Talented, not to say brilliant, at whatever she put her hand to, she was nonetheless unhappy
both at home and at school, saying she wanted "to
change to another family." During the year she spent
in England, she completely recovered her balance. She
is her own self now, no longer simply the daughter of
the man in the wheelchair. When she comes home from
school she runs to her father, with whom she is once
again as thick as in her earliest years. Like him, she
loves soccer, and together they watch the matches on
TV. Of the three children, she is the only one who
knows and uses the code perfectly. The other two will
interpret a bit from time to time, but they prefer the
words on the computer or a smiling, wordless complicity.

Looking at things positively, as we try to do, the
children can at least claim that their father is around
a great deal, which is more than most of their friends
can say! And that he has an unchallenged authority,
though it was not easy to restore.

When Philippe came home from the hospital he
was obviously not focused on his role as a father; he
was much more interested in being taken care of and
catered to than participating in family life. To compel
him to work himself back into his paternal role little
by little, whenever the children asked me about something, I would tell them to check with their father, and
soon the habit became second nature to them. His

decisions, like those of Moses, come down in writing and are therefore law. It is either yes or no, without further comment, and the discussion is over. That doesn't stop them from trying to be a little sneaky now and then. Capucine learned very quickly to turn and walk away whenever she found that the code she was interpreting contained a tongue-lashing for her.

It sometimes seems to me that I have the least attractive role in all this. I am always the one who yells, who puts her foot down, who gives orders, who is responsible for discipline. When the children are bad, Philippe's reaction is often to laugh at their behavior, or write out a reproach on his computer that, reaching them in the fullness of time, has little effect. Or else I am the one entrusted with the unhappy task of passing on his reprimands. But by the time I have translated Philippe's code, one of the three children, profiting from the fact that my concentration is elsewhere, will have turned the situation upside down. That's life. Our life.

Today Capucine, Juliette, and Pierre are wonderful children, lively and well-balanced, happy to be alive. When we go out as a family, I like their way of clustering around their father, sticking next to his wheelchair, showing they are proud of him and want to protect him. In this I see the tangible proof that our love has succeeded in overcoming every obstacle put in our way. It is also a reason to go on.

The House

ABOUT THREE MONTHS AFTER THE ACCIDENT, foreseeing that Philippe might in the long run be coming back home to live, my parents-in-law had encouraged me to move. Our roughly 750 square feet of space would unquestionably be too small for the wheelchair and all the other medical equipment indispensable to my husband's comfort. My father-in-law, who was the kind of man to make rapid decisions and put them into effect within the half hour, had persuaded me to buy an apartment in a building still under construction on the banks of the Seine, which would become available for occupancy in eighteen months. I had bought the apartment the way you buy a refrigerator, and had more or less summarily modified the existing plans to fit our needs. As for the rest, we would deal with it when the time came.

Fifteen months after this lightning purchase, I was on the train back to Paris after a stay in the mountains at Les Arcs, when I had one of those brainstorms for which I am famous. We would *not* go and live in this new apartment. Never. I only half-liked it, we would always be struggling with problems of getting in and out of the elevator (I hated to think what would happen when it was under repair). Besides, the apartment was too small. I had bought it when we were a family of four, but soon there would be five of us. My mind was made up: What we needed was a house.

The day I got back I rushed over to the hospital and, without even so much as saying hello to Philippe, began filling him in on my sudden inspiration. It was March 1992 and in June he was supposed to move home for good. The pill had to have been a bitter one for him to swallow, but he accepted it without reproaching me in any way. He must have known just as well as I how much space we were going to need from now on. To give him as much comfort as possible, I promised to start looking through the classified ads and calling real estate agencies immediately.

Eliminating Paris itself out of hand, I combed the suburbs for a full month, searching for a little corner of paradise. I gave up the idea of Saint-Cloud and Suresnes (too hilly); if ever Philippe made the slightest wrong move with his wheelchair, he ran the risk of rolling down into the Seine. In Neuilly the prices were so exorbitant you could assume the houses came equipped with bathroom fixtures of solid gold, something we could do very nicely without. The suburb of Rueil was full of speed bumps, and the sidewalks of the neighboring suburbs were all too narrow for a wheelchair. There is a decided disadvantage to being disabled in an environment exclusively designed for the hale and hearty.

It was a classified ad I happened to see that brought me to Levallois, where I first visited an old one-family house, then another — the house we live in today. A one-story house, with a little garden, it struck me as ideal, but the price was beyond our means. Nevertheless, thanks to the help of both our families, we were able to sign the purchase agreement on May 15, 1992, and take possession on July 15. In early August major construction began. That was all we needed! Pierre had just been born, we were on vacation at our house in the Allier, but as Garches Hospital refused to readmit Philippe we had no idea where Philippe would go in September. And now I had somehow managed to get involved with a wild project, adding further stress to a situation already, to say the least, stressful enough. But I was not about to give up. Throughout the entire month of August, aroused from my sleep first by Pierre then by Philippe, I would wake up to find the phone ringing and some workmen on the other end asking me questions about the new roof, ending any thought I might have had of getting a good night's sleep.

It was thanks to his sister that Philippe was finally admitted to Kerpape rehabilitation center, while work was being completed on our new house. The prospect of being exiled to Brittany did not exactly delight Philippe, and there were long and painful negotiations between us prior to his departure. He suspected me of trying to send him away, of wanting to get rid of him. But why would I ever do such a thing? For six long months I had been driving myself mercilessly, dividing my energies between the construction, the children, and weekends with Philippe. That left me precious little time for misbehaving, if that's what he was worrying about! The warm welcome Philippe received from the staff at Kerpape, and the progress he made toward autonomy during his stay there, quickly put an end to any lingering discord between us.

To top it all off, I was forced to give up our apartment in Neuilly a month before we were supposed to move into our house in Levallois, and so I suddenly found myself cooped up in a tiny studio with the three children. Pierre's snoring was so loud that none of us was able to catch a wink of sleep, the situation was rapidly becoming apocalyptic, and by the end of the second week I was ready for the loony bin. To solve the problem, we packed Pierre off to stay with my mother once again, and Capucine went to live with a friend. I kept Juliette with me and tried to get a little sleep.

The construction on our house was finished just in time, and two days before our grand move six of us household fairies arrived with our brooms, our vacuum cleaners, and dust cloths, cleaning, polishing, buffing. During the afternoon of January 30, 1993, just as we had finished installing the carpet and cleaning the windows, Philippe arrived. The following evening I organized a surprise party, gathering together everyone who had helped us in one way or another during the previous two and a half years. These social activities doubtless seemed premature to Philippe, but to me they were symbolic: They represented the start of a new life.

It may have been insanity on my part, but if I had it to do all over again, I wouldn't hesitate for a second. This house marked a major step in *our* collective recovery. For more than two years, the hospital had been our sole preoccupation. Two years of cramped and sinister rooms, which neither the children's photographs nor posters of sailboats could make cheerful. Two years of cold, ugly furniture set against a backdrop of pale, watery walls. Two years of ether smells, of endless corridors, of embarrassing lack of privacy. Two years in a world where everything assaults the eye, as though one's pain and feeling of helplessness were not enough. For those reasons, the whole house was designed by me, with the help of my architect brother, to make us forget those years as much as possible, as well as Philippe's disability. We went to great lengths to find clever ways of making it easier to get around in a wheelchair, and also allow us to conceal all the equipment and various apparatuses that he needs. For instance, a large storage cabinet adjacent to our bedroom enables us to stow the wheelchair away at night so that we don't have to stare at "that" as we fall asleep. These are the details that make a crucial difference in one's quality of life. The result: Our house is beautiful, roomy, light, airy, comfortable, and soothing. It is a place people both pass through and gather, open to movement and full of life. Each time I open the door, I feel a sense of calm and pleasure, no matter how hard a day I've had. And if I come home exhausted and my nerves on edge, I take refuge in the garden where, for a half hour, I become engrossed, or seem to be engrossed, in planting and weeding. Everyone knows that, at these times, I am not under any condition to be disturbed. When I put down my shovels and rakes and leave the laurels and the gentians behind, I am finally up to facing my tribe.

We held our housewarming party six months after we had moved in. It provided us with an opportunity to renew contact with all the many people who had not

seen Philippe since his accident and to brave their
looks, which was often a painful experience. The
"inner circle" of loyal friends had come to see him
immediately after his accident; others, however, had
held off for all sorts of reasons: because he was in
intensive care, because he might not have been feeling
up to a visit, and, to be completely honest, because I
did not want them to see Philippe in his present state.
And what a state it was! Back then he was frightening
to look at. I had more or less managed to get used to
it, but I know that some people were horribly shocked.
No matter how much I warned people, no matter how
much I prepared them ahead of time, the reality was
always much worse than my descriptions. One of
Philippe's colleagues from work insisted on going to
see him at Garches, but he never came back a second
time and now confines himself to phoning from time
to time. As for the engineer from Matra, who came to
see Philippe to figure out what kind of computer
accommodation he would need, he has only recently
confessed to me that after his visit he had spent a half
hour in the parking lot, sitting at the wheel of his car,
unable to turn on the ignition.

Six months after his return home, Philippe's face
was already much better; but it was still an impressive
sight for those who remembered him from earlier
times: confined to his wheelchair, one eye stationary
and the other roaming wildly, a trail of spittle trickling

from the corner of his mouth. He coughed a great deal, and every time he did his whole body seemed to be wheezing.

He also laughed a great deal, and once he got going he couldn't stop. Everyone who was still convinced Philippe was no longer all there took his uncontrollable laughter as proof positive of their worst fears.

By bringing us all together at the same time, the housewarming helped me turn the corner. I now no longer took personally the pitying and embarrassing looks cast our way, which judged even as they condemned us. To cover or conceal the sadness they provoked in me, I assumed an ironic or aggressive pose. To this day, there are looks we get that sometimes move me or tear me to pieces, but they are fewer and fewer. One has no recourse when people are curious, voyeuristic, mean, or even nasty, except to respond by indifference. Or with humor. As Emmanuel says whenever anyone stares at Philippe in the street: "You're right, he can't walk. But boy, can he roll."

A Couple Again . . . Second Time Around

*A*FTER TWO AND A HALF YEARS, EVERYONE was looking forward to Philippe's return home. Happiest of all of course was Philippe himself. Even if he never complained, he had to be close to the breaking point after all those months of loneliness, discomfort, and miscomprehension at the hospital. But the doctors and nurses were also glad to be relieved of an overly cumbersome patient and his omnipresent, and therefore somewhat burdensome, entourage. And I was also pleased, exhausted as I was from my disruptive life, the constant trips to and from the hospitals, the battles with the medical staff. In fact, I was so exhausted that our reunion was less idyllic than we might have hoped. Fatigue, by a large margin, won out over joy.

But this was no time for sleep! Although Pierre had been sleeping through the night for several months now, the same could not be said for Philippe. He would wake me up several times a night, usually with a plugged tracheotomy, which I had to clean out if I didn't want to find him asphyxiated the following morning. During his first weeks home I managed to fall asleep again, but then, as my fatigue and irritation grew, I could no longer go back to sleep. My memory of that period is a veritable obsession and recurring fear of being woken up at night, and everyone knows that to arouse me from the arms of Morpheus for no good and valid reason is taking their life in their hands. If Philippe catches a cold, I repair to another room to sleep, and the children know they'd best wait until morning to have their little problems sorted out. Just the other day, when a friend asked if she could leave her daughter with me, my response was, "Fine, just as long as she doesn't spend the night." Sleeping like a log is still the best way I've discovered to recharge my batteries a bit. And not thinking about a thing until morning.

My nerves on edge, I found everything and anything a pretext for impatience, testiness, or aggression. Having for two years grown accustomed, in spite of myself, to being a single parent, I now found myself adjusting with difficulty to living again as a couple, particularly as our new roles were still ill-defined: Philippe was physically present, but he was having a tough time taking part in family life again. He would just sit there, saying nothing, happy simply to watch and smile, observing everything as though trying to make up for lost time. I wanted him to spell me; here he was a burden. In the early days, his one and only pastime was watching television. From morning till evening, for hours and hours on end, he used his "James" to channel-surf, showing a marked preference for sports channels. I understood that his immobility might condemn him to this nonactivity, but I have always been of the opinion that too much television softens the brain. And since I had married a guy who was not totally unintelligent, I had no intention of winding up with a moron. Furthermore, I did not like the sound of the television as a constant background noise that permeated the house. Interpreting Philippe while a blabbermouth journalist goes endlessly on about a penalty kick requires a level of concentration that far exceeded my patience — and still does!

His escapism via TV did not distract him from his main interest: He wanted to know everything I said or did. Was it because he needed me to bring him some local color and gossip from the outside world? Or because he was afraid of being left alone, even if

Emmanuel was by now a perfectly efficient helper? Or was he jealous? In any case, I felt myself under surveillance, and I interpreted his questions as betraying a lack of confidence in me. "Who are you getting dressed up for?" he would often ask me when he saw me getting ready to go out. As if he didn't have more than enough reasons to feel terrible, he had to torture himself further by imagining that I was having an affair! I have no idea whether my explanations — some gentle, some less so — finally reassured him, but I hope that his own lucidity, which sometimes borders on cynicism, in the long run succeeded in laying his doubts to rest. In all objectivity, my hectic schedule did not leave me the slightest opening for a lover!

To put an end to Philippe's badgering questions, I drew up detailed accounts of my absolutely mad days. At 10:00 A.M., I took down my bicycle, 10:10 I arrived at the supermarket, where I bought three packages of butter, two boxes of diapers, and twenty-five rolls of paper towel. . . . When he saw me arrive with my list, Philippe gave up trying to know everything down to the last detail. But I still felt suffocated. I had to take care of the children, find a baby-sitter, a nurse, a physical therapist, an occupational therapist, plow through stacks of paperwork, interpret, organize, plan, administer, set up our own hospital at home. . . . I don't think I have ever cried so much. Putting this whole complex infrastructure into place was a full-time job, and Philippe's presence added an element of the Inquisition to the whole exercise. There were times when I came to regret my former bachelor life, unfettered and free of material constraints, when I could go to the movies or visit friends on a whim without having to consult anyone, when I could settle down on my bed with a pile of magazines, a book, the television, and the telephone. . . . Habits, whether they are good or bad, are quickly acquired. As for myself, I must have a natural tendency, which my life experience has only reinforced, for regaling myself with a thousand mindless pleasures. I was having to learn all over again how to share everything and not feel that I was losing some precious freedom, even if it was accompanied by a sense of loneliness that was sometimes terrifying.

Two months after his return home, I told Philippe I was no longer going to feed him myself. By this time, the only meal I was presiding over was breakfast, but what with getting the children up and off to school, dealing with the arrival of the day nurse and Emmanuel, for me it was still too much. Philippe thought it was already too little. My emancipation proclamation struck him as a deliberate attempt to put some distance between us, to fob him off on others, and to take less and less care of him myself. The battle between us was brutal. How could I explain to him that my decision was not based solely on my enormous ego, or a complete indifference to his welfare? The truth is, I felt no calling as a nurse or a medical helper, both positions that tend to instill relations of dependence and infantilization — which I am constantly trying to fend off. My mother may have been the one to put the bee in my bonnet. One day when she phoned, I told her I did not have any time to talk, because I was in the middle of feeding Philippe. As if I were feeding a child. With a great deal of tact, Mother pointed out to me that I could have put it quite differently. I could for instance have said that Philippe was having lunch. She would have understood and I would have spared myself from taking on the mind-set and role of his nanny. I was and am Philippe's wife, and I intend to remain so. For that I forbid myself, unless it is absolutely necessary, from playing any of the roles that look as if they're a display of tenderness and devotion but insidiously kill love.

To escape the house, under a pretext my jailer would buy, I had to find a pursuit he would respect enough not to short circuit; otherwise, each time I tried to go out, he would drum up some emergency to make me stay home! There was only one solution: to go back to work. In fact, it had been he who, in another life, had urged me to enter the work force. By the time Capucine was born, I had just received my degree and aspired to be nothing more than a young stay-at-home mother. "Stop for a while if you want, but eventually do go to work or you'll always regret it," Philippe had said. Now I saw his earlier advice as a kind of premonition.

I had the good fortune to be hired by a former client of mine to handle financial communications. Moreover, the work terms were ideal, enabling me to see to it that the house would keep running more or less properly: three days a week, slightly more during busy periods, and I would have all school holidays off. I started in October 1993 and have not stopped since. During those years my job has evolved, and I have changed positions. I love my work, partly because of the independence it gives me and partly because it provides me with an indispensable contact with the outside world. On the one hand there is home, and on the other work. Each gives me a perspective on the other. Philippe's accident has taught me to prioritize emergencies, put disasters in perspective, and even though I give my all to my work, I know that my life is not at stake. Yet I also know that there is a world outside of our home, and that I have my place in it.

And What About Me?

WHY DID I STAY? OUT OF LOVE, and also out of duty. Perhaps I could have left and delegated to others — to my parents-in-law, for instance — the task of taking care of their son. But the thought never even crossed my mind. If I stayed, it is because there had been eight years of love before the accident, eight years forming a bond strong enough to withstand this seismic event of a force far beyond the Richter scale.

The urge to throw everything over does hit me at regular intervals, but no sooner does it arrive than it immediately subsides. I would never have the courage: I have fought too hard here ever to think of starting again anywhere else. So, without asking myself any further questions, I stay and hold fast, my eyes wide open. "Hell surely exists," I found myself telling a little girl one day who was curious about death after hearing about it at school, "but it is right here on earth."

How did I survive this "hell"?

I had a wonderful support system, and an enormous supply of friendship and generosity. But at the same time I also felt incredibly lonely, knowing that I couldn't share my feelings with anyone, not even my closest friends. No one could ever imagine my anguish, understand the pressures I was under and the tension I felt at every moment of every day. With a few people, I did allow myself to give way to tears. But I am not very good at tears, and whenever I start to feel them welling up, I chase them away by a round of hyperactivity, which is more in keeping with my temperament! On the other side of the coin, I sometimes find myself floored by indescribable bouts of fatigue. This is my way of being paralyzed, of saying "Stop — enough," of being at the end of my rope, incapable of either acting or speaking. There are times — sometimes long periods — when I remain as if in a trance, in a state of utter exhaustion, and if the earth were to collapse I would not move a muscle. After which I'll get up and off I'll go again, often thanks to the children, who inform me with some of their energy.

★　　★　　★

During the first two months, I thought only of Philippe: My prime and indeed sole concern was that he come out of his coma and avoid the worst. Then I had to think of Capucine and Juliette. And, finally, I had to think of myself, for the simple reason that I was not alone and that if I wanted life to go on I would have to be constantly on my toes, prepared for any eventuality.

Thinking about myself meant resorting to a thousand different things that might bring me a semblance of well-being. First there were massage sessions to relax my tense body. Then visits to the chiropractor to realign my back after the very special strains it suffered from transferring Philippe from the bed to the wheelchair and back again. Then yoga, to learn breathing and sharpen my synapses. And energy therapy, to get my energies circulating throughout my body. Each of these methods was effective in its own way, although I generally tended to follow them for a while and then give up. My body, a very effective barometer when my head refused to recognize its own limits, would let me know when I had had enough of carrying everything on my own shoulders, both literally and figuratively.

To give voice to my suffering, which I otherwise repressed, and vent some of the rage, rebellion, and confusion that were threatening to do me in, I went to a psychoanalyst for some three years, which helped me put a little order in my chaos. As necessary as this step may have been, it did nothing to change reality: I was married to a handicapped person, I had three children, and I had to accept responsibility. It was my choice; no one had forced me to stay.

Moving on from the unconscious to the irrational, I consulted several fortune-tellers and astrologers. If indeed they may see the present clearly enough, they often have trouble predicting the future. But they all promised me, without asking my opinion, that I would have a number of highs and lows in the years to come! While it may not have been exactly a revelation, they offered me the reassurance that, as far as the cards and stars were concerned, Philippe would live. One even went so far as to predict that I would live to a peaceful and ripe old age. If only he knew how much the image of being an adoring grandmother meant to me at the time! I believed it without believing in it, but in our situation one overlooked nothing: prayer circles, figures of the saints, little handkerchiefs moistened in holy water from the shrine at Lourdes. . . .

More seriously and concretely, if I am to avoid cracking up, I have to get away. Alone, that is, without any member of my family, but together with a girlfriend. To recharge my batteries, return to my roots, and, miracle of miracles, do nothing, absolutely nothing, but relax, revel in the color of the flowers, the beauty of the landscapes, the sweetness of things. Whenever I do escape, I finally get a chance to profit from the passage of time without having to control the course of events.

The first time I raised the idea of getting away, in May 1991, Philippe and I had a terrible row. He was furious, accusing me of abandoning him, and I was not as sanguine about the whole notion as I pretended. It took long negotiations and a strong dose of willpower on my part to resist giving in to his arguments and persist in leaving after all. My weary organism took its revenge: A horrendous sore throat ruined my first getaway to a saltwater spa at La Baule, a getaway during which Philippe had his sister call me every day to make sure I didn't forget him. But it would have taken a lot more than that to convince me not to repeat the experiment.

So I do make an effort to get away regularly. In theory, I allow myself two absences a year, but in practice I often miss one! Yet these interludes are indispensable, I now realize; I know myself well enough to sense when it is time to bestir myself and go. It's either that or draping a veil over my face and stopping up my ears.

These moments of self-imposed solitude are all the more necessary as Philippe is always at home. To some degree, that makes up for the vacations we used to take together when he was well.

There is, I am sure, a great deal of egoism in all this, but there is also the humility to recognize that I am not indispensable. For a long time I thought that nothing would work if I weren't there, I wanted to be in charge, to control and direct everything. As time went on, I have learned how to delegate, to keep my perspective, and I have also become fatalistic. For better or worse, what will happen will happen whether or not I am there. The worst might happen just as easily on a day when I am out window-shopping in Paris. And so I say, *Inshallah! It's in the hands of God.* I hesitate, find all sorts of excuses to put off my trip or cancel it altogether, but the day when I finally make up my mind, nothing can stand in my way and I immediately feel better. Even the prospect of these few, privileged moments brings light to my horizon.

As scandalous as it may seem, I call home once, to announce my safe arrival, but after that, complete silence. This habit evolved out of an incident from an earlier trip. After I had gone to great lengths just to find a telephone booth in some isolated corner of Greece, Philippe, furious because he was upset by some detail of my return schedule, made poor Emmanuel hang up the phone. Since then, I have taken pains to protect myself from these mood swings. A vacation is a vacation.

The children are now used to my periodic absences and don't hold them against me. If they await my return with bated breath, it's as much for the chance to rifle through my bags looking for the presents I've brought as it is the pleasure of seeing me again. Once I close the house door behind me, I no longer give either the children or Philippe a second thought. Philippe is getting better all the time and has amply proved that he is a kind of colossus able to cope with anything. Before I leave I no longer bother to fill the refrigerator and the cupboards with food, draw up lists of doctors in case this or that happens . . . or find backup help. Emmanuel and Leila are there to make sure things run smoothly during the day, and our friends Louis and Annick move in at night, reveling in their premature role of indulgent grandparents, and turn our room into a gambling hall where Philippe and they play endless hands of blackjack.

Louis solemnly claims in any case that "absence makes the heart grow fonder." Louis is a philosopher, and his wisdom, grounded in generosity, is made up of equal parts kindness, humor, and extraordinary intuition.

In the periods between two solitary escapades, I have learned to carve out some time for myself, no matter what, and to preserve my hard-fought moments of freedom. For almost a decade, what with all the battles I had to fight, the challenges to meet, the hospitals, the construction work, the complications, I lived in a state of constant anxiety. Absorbed in the task of rebuilding a more or less normal life, I too in my own way gradually shut myself off from the world. I would get up in the morning, my face a cold mask, a deep worry line etched on my forehead, like an ageless crone, worn to a nub, bone weary. A few years ago, a friend who had come to spend some time with us at our country house was kind enough to sound the alarm:

"You're growing hard, Stéphane, you're letting yourself get too wrapped up in all this." I can never thank her enough for having opened my eyes: If I was to go on, I had to learn how and when to stop!

That same year I started playing golf and riding horseback again, sports that I love but had given up after the accident. During vacation that year I forced myself to leave the house from 4:00 to 7:00 P.M., to whack at a golf ball. Between the children's recriminations ("What! You're going out again?") and Philippe's reproaches ("You would really do anything *not* to take care of me, wouldn't you?"), you really had to be motivated. The inner peace that I found on the golf course, striding along its tree-bordered fairways, convinced me to stand my ground, and nothing could ever persuade me to give up golf.

It is equally impossible for me to imagine my life without the pleasures and benefits I draw from my handicrafts. Picture framing and porcelain painting bring me an irreplaceable feeling of peace, which I have no intention of giving up, even if Philippe teases me about my middle-class hobbies. What does it matter if I become almost a caricature of the happy bourgeois housewife? I enjoy these moments when I get together with my friends over a cup of coffee and talk about whatever comes into our heads, as much as I enjoy the satisfaction of working with my hands. The results can be seen in my china. I need to create, even if what I create seems silly.

Thanks to these various diversions and hobbies, I have carved out for myself a space that belongs exclusively to me, and I have stopped resenting the feeling that my life was so restricted. If we're to have some degree of equilibrium, all of us need this kind of independence, which has helped me return to my own age. Today I feel thirty-something again, even if I have the impression that I already have fifty lives behind me.

Pratfalls and Laughter

You DON'T NEED A LICENSE TO PUSH A WHEELCHAIR. And yet handling one is a long, slow learning process, which requires a solid knowledge not only of the machine itself but of the terrain you're dealing with. Wheelchair training should begin with intensive exercise sessions and an introduction to basic mechanics. If one of the tires is improperly inflated, the wheelchair becomes twice as heavy. And when every crack or mound on the sidewalk takes on Himalayan proportions, you can see the usefulness of having well-developed biceps.

To give our muscles a well-deserved rest and continue our march toward progress, for a time we used an electric wheelchair. The children had a ball with it, but after it got out of control two or three times and threatened to slam Philippe into a wall or send him tumbling down the stairs, we decided the illusion of freedom it offered was more than offset by our innate trust in human power rather than that of technology. Nonetheless, no matter how adroit humans may be, they are sometimes prone to moments of distraction or clumsiness.

During one of our early vacations in the Allier, Pascale and I decided to take Philippe for a walk in the woods, the ones he loves so much. We were no more than a few yards into it when we were set upon by a swarm of mosquitoes, which convinced us to go no farther, and we beat a quick retreat to the car. I'd started to raise the wheelchair on the hoist when I happened to notice my nephew stuffing Rice Krispies into his mouth and scattering them all over the car. Annoyed, I started in his direction, forgetting that someone always has to remain standing behind the wheelchair. My scolding was suddenly interrupted by a loud thud. Philippe was lying on the ground, head over heels with laughter. After our initial moments of panic, we managed to get him right side up, reasonably safe and sound, thanks no doubt to the headrest that tied his head in place and, in this instance, kept his neck from snapping back. It took Pascale and me two hours to calm down, and we made a solemn oath that in the future Philippe would have to settle for the trees in the garden. He, however, seemed delighted by our little interlude.

Each time Philippe takes a fall, our reaction is a mixture of mirth and terror. One Saturday afternoon we had decided to go to the movies. My mother was taking care of the children and my father-in-law, seeing I was running late, had offered to get Philippe settled in the car. A few moments later, while I was still primping, my mother called out urgently for help. I raced down the stairs four at a time to discover a most unusual sight: My father-in-law was screaming, the neighbors were hanging out their windows, and the wheelchair was lying on its side. . . . It had slipped off the hoist. Summoning all the strength and calm with which I fortunately seem to possess during moments of extreme panic, I managed to lift both Philippe and the wheelchair and set them upright again. His glasses were plastered onto his face, his arms showed the marks of the wheels, but once again Philippe was roaring with laughter. Between two hiccups he managed to make it clear the outing was still on. I installed him in the car and off we went, while our neighbors looked on aghast and my father-in-law, standing there in the middle of the street, looked livid. When we got home, he was stretched out on the sofa, still in a near-apoplectic state from the experience. Ever since, he has

been extremely hesitant about volunteering to help
with the wheelchair.

Even if Philippe never complains about our moments
of clumsiness and has the great good grace to respond
to our mishaps with gales of laughter, it goes without
saying we do our best to avoid them. And we do try
as hard as we can to make sure he's comfortable, with
varying degrees of success, wonderfully aided and
abetted by his mechanical helpers such as his "James,"
which enables him to give commands both to his computer and to the television set, as well as to call us
whenever he needs help. The days "James" went on
the blink, we lived in a permanent state of alert, just
as in the old Garches days, hardly daring to leave
Philippe alone, since he had no way of summoning us
in case of an emergency. When, after an agonizingly
long month, James was finally repaired, it once again
became our incomparable ally, and we respond to its
call immediately if not sooner.

All this does not alter the fact that a person with
locked-in syndrome requires a very special kind of
attention. Since Philippe can't communicate verbally,
he has to count on our ability to see the problem, but
even after considerable training it's often hard to com-
prehend what is going on at first glance. When suddenly I see Philippe bobbing his head, his eyes staring
and popping out of his head, it takes me several sec-

onds to figure out the cause of his fear or pain. Sometimes his hand has slipped off the armrest and his fingers are caught in the spokes; sometimes a wasp or yellow jacket is buzzing too close to his tracheotomy. Or a fly is tickling his neck and he can't flick it away. And then there was the time when a baby carrot lovingly picked and given to him by Juliette got stuck in his throat. . . . The world is full of unsuspected dangers. In our house, even a carrot can prove fatal. The most harmless incident can turn into a nightmare. When-ever you escape or avoid one more catastrophe, you laugh at your fright of the moment before. Laughter as an escape valve.

Private Life and Public Life

PHILIPPE'S HOMECOMING INCREASED THE SIZE of our family. It wasn't that we celebrated his return by conceiving triplets, but that the new situation obliged us to bring in competent and reliable help.

The first one to enlarge our circle was Emmanuel. I became convinced of the need for a third person during one of Philippe's early weekends at home. Five months pregnant, I found myself trying to hoist the wheelchair onto a sidewalk full of cracks, with Capucine on one side and Juliette perched on her father's knees, as still as a mummy for fear of falling. A light went on that day, convincing me not only that I was at the end of my rope, but also that if I were even to try and go any farther I was in for a bad fall. Whence the necessity of hiring somebody to give me a hand with Philippe. But who?

A combination of luck and chance brought Emmanuel our way. When I put in my call to a personnel agency, he just happened to be sitting across the desk from the woman taking my call and said he was interested in my position. So it was that in March 1992 he came to us. He began by working weekends, then joined us for our summer vacation in the Allier, where he was (almost) present for Pierre's birth, after which he went on to Kerpape, since Philippe refused to go there without him. Finally, he followed us to Levallois where, every day from 9:00 A.M. to 6:00 P.M., he is both Philippe's companion and his scapegoat, his confidant, his go-between, his arms, his hands. . . . The two form a most amazing duo. The Smith & Wesson of Levallois! With all the ups and downs of any couple. Above all, an enormous complicity, but there are also arguments, pouting, and heavy silences, but ultimately they are inseparable. To complete the picture, I should add that the children and I immediately adopted Emmanuel, and that he seems to have reciprocated.

Leila joined our special little club roughly six months later. I had put an ad in the local paper in the Allier, and among the dozen or so candidates I interviewed, she was my favorite. And yet she was hardly the image of a typical nanny. Young and pretty, a slender brunette wearing skintight stretch pants and perched on high heels, she did not seem to have the build for the heavy work I had in mind for her: to take care of the three children when I was away and keep a big house spic and span. The prospect didn't seem to frighten her. She had gone to secretarial school but was tired of working on things that didn't interest her and had decided to devote herself to what she truly liked, which was taking care of children. Sweeping and dusting did not frighten her in the least. My hunch proved correct: For all her seeming fragility, Leila is indefatigable. And strong. If you doubt my words, you simply have to see her toting crates of paper towels and mineral water, which Philippe consumes in enormous quantities.

Whoever said you don't choose your family? Ours was built and modeled very happily. Emmanuel and Leila are an integral part of the family. They are the second engine of our household, which would barely function without them, if at all. Through their virtues of sensitivity and intuition, they are part and parcel of our life and yet always discreet, not an easy task in our house, where there are no hidden agendas: What you see is what you get. They are participants, and they are also witnesses in spite of themselves. Both of them are privy to everything that goes on between us, acting not only as extensions of ourselves but as mediators, a strategic role that each of us plays in turn: Emmanuel mediates between Philippe and me, Leila between the children and me, Emmanuel between the children and Philippe, I between Philippe and Emmanuel, and so on. Lord knows, our high-pressure family relationships need regularly to be defused!

Over the months and years, we have learned to live together, to give and take, and to accept one another's foibles. I may have raised bloody hell a few times when I could not find some object in the exact place I had put it, but these details are insignificant compared to the bonds that unite us.

Around this solid nucleus, a number of satellites gravitate: Pierre, the physical therapist; Gilles and Jacqueline, the nurses who spell each other off each day, when Philippe wakes and when he goes to bed; a speech pathologist; and Patrick, the yoga teacher. There are others, too, who fill in for Emmanuel at night and on weekends. . . . Were I to name them all, it would almost sound like the training program for some stressed-out "golden boy." Except that, in our case, the program is operative year round, and the so-called luxury is essential simply to maintain Philippe's body, to retain its suppleness, to gain a hundredth of a millimeter of movement. These "satellites," who have now become our friends, are indispensable to

Philippe, and their regular and frequent visits have created certain bonds. Complicity, but also friction. One day I found myself running out into the street to catch up with one of them because Philippe had made some nasty remark, because of which he had threatened to quit. At least you have to admit there is never a dull moment! There are constant comings and goings, and talk, and giggles, and motion, and squabbling. There's life, a life full of color — a little too much at times — but, when all is said and done, there is joy.

Our numerous friends keep the house in a state of perpetual motion. There are those who stop in to have lunch with Philippe, those who come to play bridge, those who bring news of the outside world and take the opportunity to solicit Philippe's valued advice, those who call before they come, those who drop in unexpectedly, those who have been there since the beginning, those who have turned up when we were least expecting them, those we would probably never have met had this whole thing not happened. . . . All those who have proven their generosity, their heart, their open-mindedness. What a family!

Although it was never planned, I find this communal life quite attractive in many ways, and if one day it were to stop, I'm pretty sure I would miss it. But the other side of the coin is that it's hard to find either the time or the space for any kind of private life. It's only after 8:30 in the evening that we become a "normal" couple again, just the two of us, rather than four, six, eight, or more. It can get crowded. A chosen crowd, a beloved crowd, whose caring and affection are constantly precious to us, but a crowd that sometimes gives me the impression that my life is being played out in front of an audience. It isn't all that easy to wake up in the morning and find some outside person already there, but that's the way things are. I live with it, and I keep reminding myself: either I take over as nurse or I put up with this other presence. But there are times when I blow up.

My sister-in-law Pascale, my ally and accomplice, one day bore the full brunt of my pent-up emotions. During the time Philippe was at Garches, we were so close that the medical staff started to call us the "Tigresses." Whether together or alone, we were informed with the same stubbornness, the same determination, the same burning desire to make sure things changed and Philippe was better cared for. More than once, Pascale has also played the role of a messenger between her brother and me. When I was so tied up I couldn't get to the hospital, she was the only one who could make him listen to reason and keep him from overdramatizing: I wasn't there not because I was trying to shirk my duty but because of an unavoidable conflict. It was also Pascale who spelled me at home once when I had to go away for several days. To make certain there would be no nocturnal accident, she moved into our bedroom — in fact, she slept in our bed. When I heard about it, I was furious: She may have been trying to do the right thing, but in my eyes she had overstepped the bounds and entered what I believe must always remain a private preserve. My violent reaction must have hurt her, but it serves as a good illustration of one of the contradictions in my life: the impossibility of doing without others in the conduct of my daily affairs, and my strong desire for a private life, sheltered from all eyes.

Where is the frontier between sharing your life with others and making a spectacle of yourself? My natural reticence has made me take our public life as a reason not to indulge in any histrionics — which are in any case foreign to me — and has made me loath to show myself in a light that, because of fatigue and impatience, is not always flattering. My attitude tells a lot more about me than do any secrets I might reveal. I had trouble coming to terms with myself, accepting myself as I am, so that I don't suffer from living in a community atmosphere, however discreet and well-meaning my colleagues may be, since they see me without artifice or embellishments. I take comfort in knowing that those who love me love me as I am. Not a saint or a martyr, not a monster or a witch. As for the rest, people can think what they will, and I shall keep my secrets locked up in my soul.

Shouts and Murmurs

A PUBLIC SHOW OF GRIEF IS VERY MUCH IN STYLE. In my case what was strange was having to grieve for someone who was still there. Philippe was both the same person and someone else, a different someone I had to get used to.

Getting used to seeing his lively and expressive face become deformed, ravaged, and devoid of expression; seeing his healthy, active, and muscular body turn thin and inert, without the slightest gesture or reaction. In a few short weeks, what incredible damage! Fortunately, there were still the eyes, but how horribly painful it was to see him like this!

The worst, however, was seeing the body of the man I love treated as a public object: bandied about, carried, bumped into, examined, touched, tubed,

201

transfused, probed, hooked up, and plugged in. Though constantly monitored, his body was also oddly neglected: always sloppily dressed, two years spent in a shapeless sweat suit — I prefer to exercise in blue jeans — his teeth not brushed and his hair unwashed. For the professionals into whose care his body was entrusted, personal modesty is an abstract concept; they have no idea what seduction and desire mean, two concepts that are grounded in mystery.

Under these circumstances, I too started to manipulate his body. I cleaned him and brushed his teeth. I washed his hair, his head resting on my stomach — quite a feat when I was seven months pregnant! — with bottles of water, three towels, and two basins, one on either side, a little improvised shower, to help him recover a bit of dignity. I learned to clean a tracheotomy, rub an eye that itched. At first I was afraid I might be doing it all wrong or hurting him, but little by little I did it mechanically, like a nurse. I even became an expert at unplugging the tracheal opening with whatever objects happened to be handy: a screwdriver, a nail file, whatever. I've turned into his handyman! And the apparent roughness with which I still handle Philippe now and then never fails to draw rebukes from my entourage: "Careful there! You're going to hurt him!" But I know that I'm not hurting him. Unfortunately, I am all too familiar with what I am doing.

I should never have let myself be drawn into this whole infernal process: from caring about someone, you lose all awareness of his body, and the desire that goes with it. A wife becomes a nurse, and it's hard to shift gears back and forth from one role to the other. If I gradually gave up taking care of Philippe personally, it was not to get rid of him but to rediscover him, a husband and not a patient. To rekindle my desire for him.

It goes without saying that if ever there is an emergency or an immediate need, I am ready and able to move in and take over, but it is not an easy role. Some nights I will take care of him as a nurse, and a minute later he wants me to become his wife again, loving and desirable. To me, the two are incompatible. I do wish I could experience only the gestures of love. As I wish Philippe could make them again. Tenderness needs a palpable, a physical response.

To make up for what is inevitably missing, his no longer being able to take me in his arms, to kiss or caress me, Philippe overcompensates by showering me with a thousand little thoughtful gestures that would delight any woman. I tell him how I was unfairly reprimanded at work, which upset me to no end? Next day I receive a magnificent bouquet of flowers. My birthday is around the corner? He organizes a surprise party, at home or in a restaurant, with people I love. He suggests going for a drive? It turns out we are going to pick out a new ring for me. . . . I could give hundreds of examples. Each time, Philippe manages to surprise me.

It's obvious that I love these thoughtful gestures. But I am not always as touched as I should be. Is it because I am afraid of giving in to my emotions? For a very long time now I have kept my emotions at bay, as I never knew where they might take me! I've put so much rage into my battles that I have trouble turning it down to "low" to leave room for any other emotion.

I have grown awkward and often gruff in expressing the way I feel. At times I'm sure Philippe finds me a killjoy. When he asks me for something, I don't say, "Okay, but I don't really want to." Instead, I turn the two propositions around: I start by saying I'd prefer not to, then I say "Fine, I'll do it." That's become a reflex, not a very pleasant one I agree, but you have to admit there are attenuating circumstances! The enthusiasm and sense of initiative I could readily accept from a man standing on his own two feet is, I find, much harder to take from a man who is sitting and doesn't move. Any project he dreams up and "talks" me into doing inevitably adds to my workload. I'll have to make the phone calls, offer explanations, set up and attend meetings, translate or interpret. . . . My initial reaction is always to complain, although I eventually end up acquiescing because I'm happy to see him active in his own way, full of imagination, making plans. At those times, I recall the character traits I found so seductive in him in our earlier life. But I would be hard-pressed to ever express all this concretely, or to a third party.

Just as they sap all desire, hospitals strip you of tenderness and the words to express it. I never forced myself to quell these feelings, but circumstances never gave me the time to give them voice, either. Because you arrive in a hospital room where there are already several other people, be they nurses or patients; because you are caught up in a whole host of practical and material details; because emergencies demand efficiency more than flights of lyricism; because. . . . And before you know it, you lose your actual ability to talk about love. Not that you don't think about it: When Philippe "spoke" for the first time in code, I can swear that the letters spelled I-L-O-V-E-Y-O-U. He insists that he was saying F-O-O-T (to complain about his foot being in an uncomfortable position) and refuses to concede I was right! Not that it matters. Because ever since then, Philippe, who always considered that his love was obvious enough not to require words, has never missed an opportunity to tell me, even to write me, that he loves me.

In moments of anger, I have often thought I would have preferred that he stop loving me, or love me less than before, which would have made it easier for me to leave him. I must have told him as much, for when

I lose my temper, I'm usually mean, out of control, sometimes cruel. Philippe has the gift of pushing me to the brink like no one else. He also has the ability to bring out the best in me, as well as the worst. The worst are my verbal outbursts, which nothing and no one can prevent. It takes very little to set them off: the sound of him grinding his teeth a little too noisily, the tracheotomy-coughing happening once too often. One day when we were on our way to the movies, just seeing him in trousers that were covered with food stains from the night before made me hysterical. What an earful I gave the poor man! Yet I knew full well it wasn't he who had dressed himself, and that he had considered it wasn't worth picking a fight with the woman who was replacing Emmanuel that day and was in charge of getting him dressed. In any case, it's always Philippe I take it out on, for his as well as everyone else's presumed peccadilloes, for two reasons: One, he is always there, and two, I think he's the only one who can really understand me, because he doesn't answer back, or only after a delay. Tough luck for him.

At what point do you start feeling guilty? The question is always at the back of my mind, and I am often tortured by doubt and self-questioning: I should have done this, I shouldn't have done that, I was nasty, I have no right to act this way. . . . But you have to know when to stop berating yourself — and also identifying with others. I don't want to put myself in Philippe's place: Every time I try to, I get a big lump in my throat, as well as in my stomach and head, and I have to hammer away at it to make it disappear. The lump has all the weight of his great loss, a loss he must often feel, and maybe always will. At first, I couldn't get rid of that lump, then . . . what was the point of crying with him? I was wasting my time. Each of us has to fight his own battles. It has nothing to do with feelings. Life is nothing but a ball of emotions. And violent emotions to boot!

Over time, Philippe and I have developed an almost telepathic communication: I know his look, what he's going to say before he even bats an eyelash. Such osmosis is often heavy, oppressive, which is why I struggled so hard to get out of the house: so I would no longer be entirely dependent on his gaze. If I hadn't taken a breather now and then, we both would have suffocated. This decision, as well as so many others, may look as though I'm usurping all the power in our relationship, but given his situation, Philippe is often forced to give in to me, as if he were at the mercy of my every whim. After the first couple of years, during which I got used to deciding everything on my own, I had to learn to accept his point of view. He had succeeded in convincing me that he had sufficient perspective to make sound decisions. And today, despite my tendency to try and bring people around to my viewpoint and arrange things in my favor, the two of us jointly make decisions.

We haven't overcome all the obstacles in our path merely to end up destroying each other by a collision of immutable forces. I have had enough of violence. Little by little, tenderness is returning, in waves that, by slow degrees, are forming little beaches.

Onward One and All!

W*HAT CAN I HAVE POSSIBLY DONE* in another life to deserve this one? How did all this happen? Why to us? These questions, which keep coming back without ever a response, can be swept away with a single, unanswerable remark: I like my lot just as it is — intense, turbulent, extreme. That I have lived like a galley slave for almost a decade has had its rewards. I have more friends than I used to, greater independence, more strength (physical as well as mental), a clearer mind, and a certain maturity. But at what cost? I have no desire to draw up a balance sheet.

I look at Philippe, and I'm proud of him. He has never wasted his energy on self-destruction; on the contrary, he has focused on rebuilding himself, with an extraordinary ability to accept his condition without, so far as I can see, rebelling against it — something that both fascinates and disturbs me. I never for a moment suspected that I was married to a wise man!

If there were ever any doubt about how far we've come, you only have to look at Philippe's face: It has been imperceptibly reshaped, measured in fractions of inches — but a fraction of an inch per month does add up to visible change. I see his old face again, which is both wonderful and upsetting. It brings back images, flashbacks that take me by surprise and go right to my heart, which results in long minutes of unbearable emotion — bringing near-tears to my eyes, which then subside, because one has to move on.

Over the years, we have stockpiled a sufficient number of memories so that we no longer have to disinter the old ones. And the time that lies ahead promises us a future. I don't want to think about it, I don't like to picture it. Our entire organization works because we are still young, energetic, resilient, but where will we find the strength to move mountains as we grow older? The only thing we know for sure is that the worst is behind us. And what still strikes outsiders as something unbelievably horrible we have managed to normalize.

Two years ago at Easter we traveled together as a family to Sicily. It was our first trip in a plane, our first vacation in an unfamiliar house, with people who hadn't been warned what they were getting into.

Everyone loved our vacation, and Philippe has only one thought in mind: to do it again. With this book behind him — a project that occupied him for several years — he is at work on another. He has plans, ideas, desires, and there are times when it occurs to me that he is actually happy.

The children are growing up.

I have just returned from several days in Greece, where I was on a "therapeutic break," my first in a year and a half, and I am preparing myself for a period of even more intense work. Meanwhile, I'm doing everything I can to find someone to take care of Philippe at night and on weekends after Emmanuel has gone home. I have lost count of how many people we have interviewed in the last nine years, but I can feel my enthusiasm waning at the prospect of explaining the whole situation again to the latest applicant. Despite which my life is becoming less and less stressed.

Tonight, our house will once again host a meeting of ALIS (the Association of Locked-in Syndrome), of which Philippe is treasurer.

Not long ago we received a letter from a man with locked-in syndrome, who sent us his best wishes and support. The letter had been typed on a computer. But at the bottom, in a shaky hand, the man had signed his name.

Hope springs eternal.